フォニックス 65 のルールで 聞ける、言え[illegible]、[illegible]る、書ける

New Active Phonics

英語の「文字と音のルール」65 を学ぼう。
フォニックスで英語の土台づくりをしよう。

聞ける 英語の音を聞き分ける。
言える 伝わりやすく発音する。
読める カタカナをふらないで自分で読む。
書ける 丸暗記しないで英語の単語を書く。

1. Phonics Alphabet

▶（フォニックスアルファベット）

Rules 1 〜 26 🔊1

アルファベットの文字１つがそれぞれ１つの音をあらわすグループ。アルファベットの文字には名前と音がある。

1 A a

口を横に開いて、
あごを下げて

apple

2 B b

くちびるを閉じて、
一気に声を出して

bear

5 E e

口を横に開いて、
指２本、にっこり

egg

6 F f

下くちびるをかんで、
息だけで

fish

9 I i

口を横に開いて、
指１本、すまし顔

ink

10 J j

d の位置から舌を
はなして

jet

13 M m

くちびるを閉じて、
鼻にぬいて

monkey

14 N n

舌先を上の前歯の裏に
つけ、鼻にぬいて

nest

17 Q q

k や c と同じ音

queen

18 R r

くちびるをつき出し
口ぶえをふくように

rabbit

21 U u

あごを上げて、
上を向いてびっくりして

umbrella

22 V v

下くちびるをかんで、
声を出して

violin

25 Y y

舌先で下の前歯をおして

yard

26 Z z

歯と歯を軽く合わせて、
声を出して

zebra

3 C c

口の奥で息だけで

cow

4 D d

舌先を上歯ぐきにつけて、
一気に声を出して

dog

7 G g

口の奥で一気に
声を出して

goat

8 H h

のどの奥から、
一気に息だけで

hat

11 K k

口の奥で一気に
息だけで

king

12 L l

舌先を上の前歯の裏に
つけて

lion

15 O o

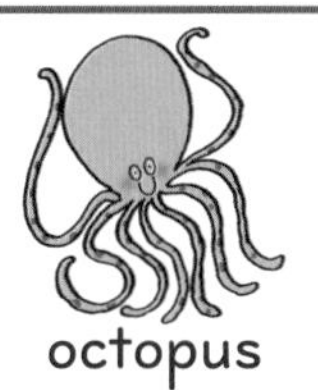

口をたてに開いて、
指 3 本、大きく

octopus

16 P p

くちびるを閉じて、
一気に息だけで

pig

19 S s

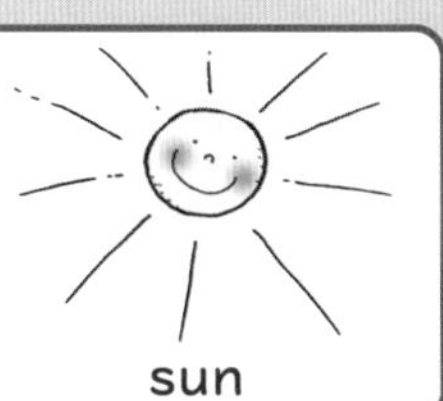

歯と歯を軽く合わせて、
息だけで

sun

20 T t

舌先を上歯ぐきにつけて、
一気に息だけで

tiger

23 W w

くちびるをつき出し、
胸の奥から r と同じ

witch

24 X x

k と s をつなげて、
息だけで

fox

Phonics Jingle
（フォニックスジングル）
A から Z まで言おう。
🔈 2 or

A says a, a, apple.

文字の名前　文字の音　キーワード

2. Consonants （子音）

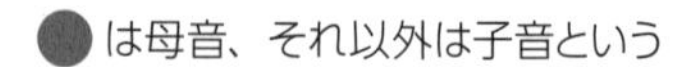

● は母音、それ以外は子音という

Experiment 🔊 3

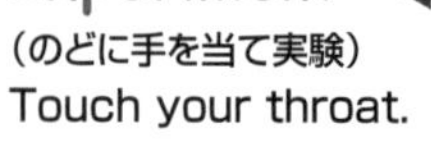

（のどに手を当て実験）
Touch your throat.

voiced sound（有声音）

のどがビリビリする。

voiceless sound（無声音）

ビリビリしない。

❶ Voiced or Voiceless?
（有声音、無声音?）

Color the voiced sound circles.
（有声音に色をぬろう。）

🔊 4

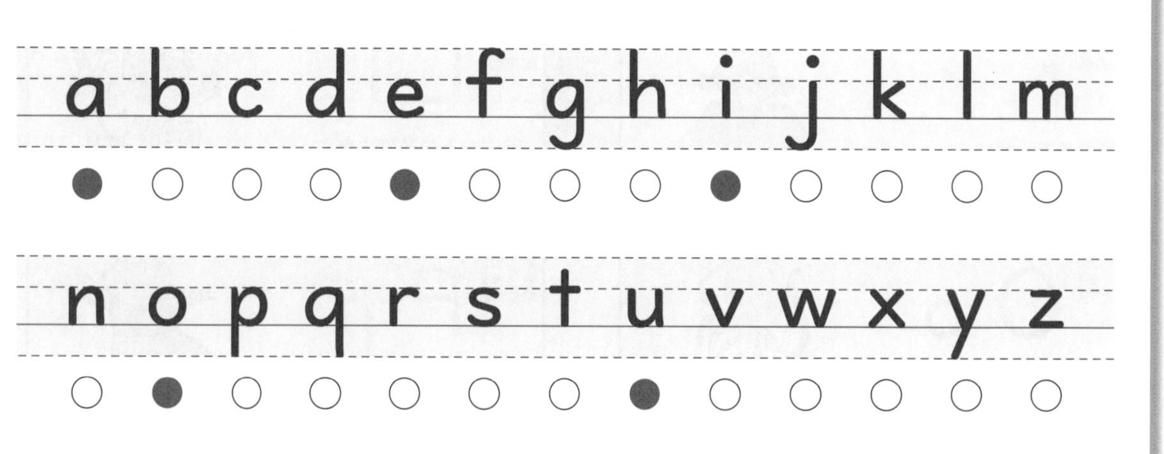

❷ Voiced or Voiceless?
（有声音、無声音?）

Color the voiceless sound circles.
（無声音に色をぬろう。）

🔊 4

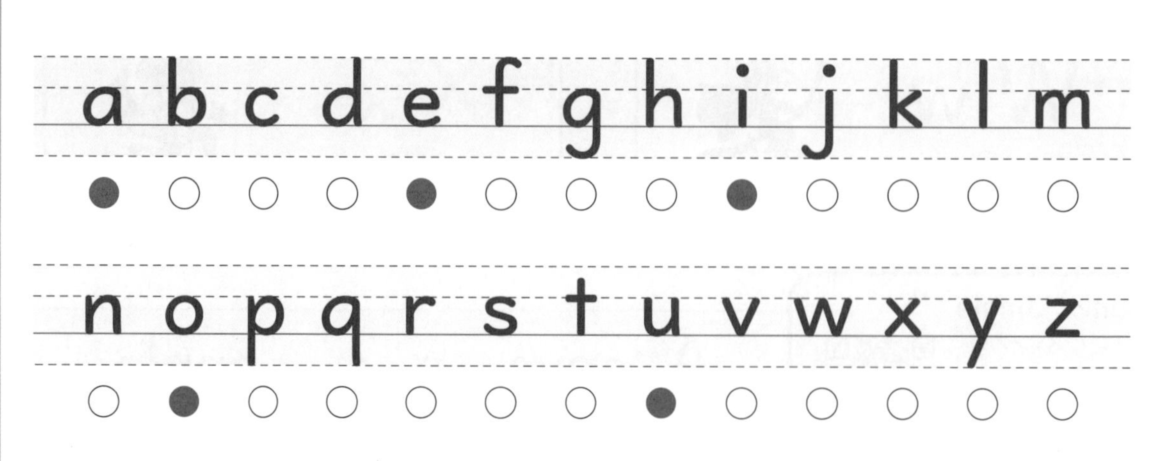

❸ Cousin Sounds Speed Speaking
（いとこ音早言い）

Point to the letters and make the sounds.
（文字を指さして、音を言おう。）

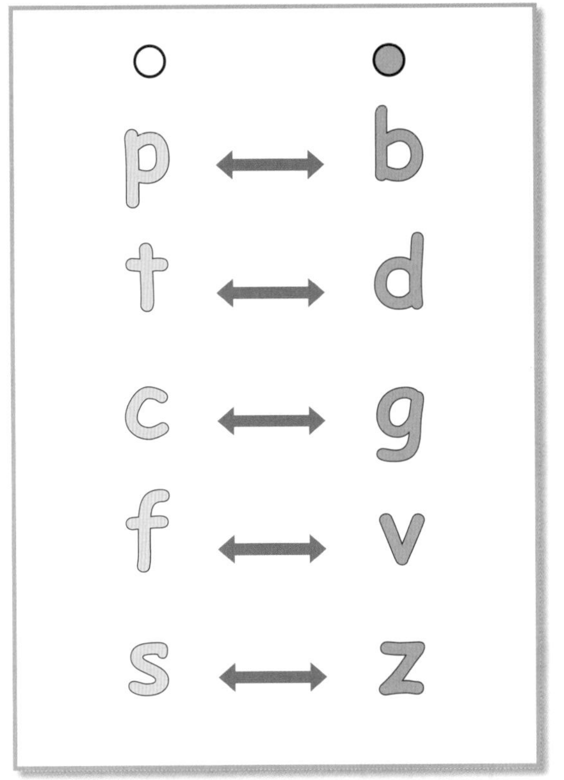

Cousin Sounds
いとこ音=口の形が同じで
有声音か無声音が違う音

❹ Initial Sound Bingo（はじめの音ビンゴ）

Write consonant letters in any of the boxes below. Listen to the Phonics Alphabet keywords(p. 2-3) and play BINGO.
（21の子音から好きな16文字を選んでビンゴカードを作り、聞こえたキーワードのはじめの音ビンゴをしよう。）

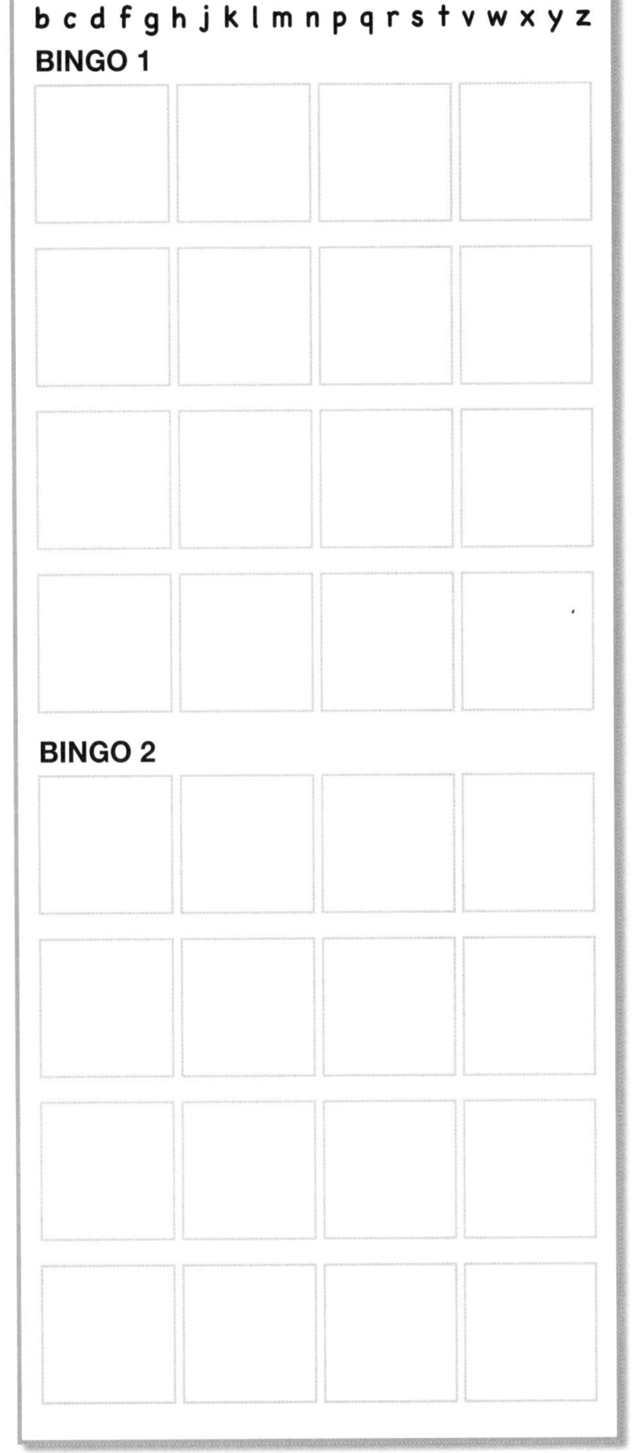

❶ Final Sound Matching
（終わりの音と文字合わせ）
Listen and match the pictures and the final sound letters with lines.
（単語を聞いて、合う絵と終わりの文字を線で結ぼう。）
5

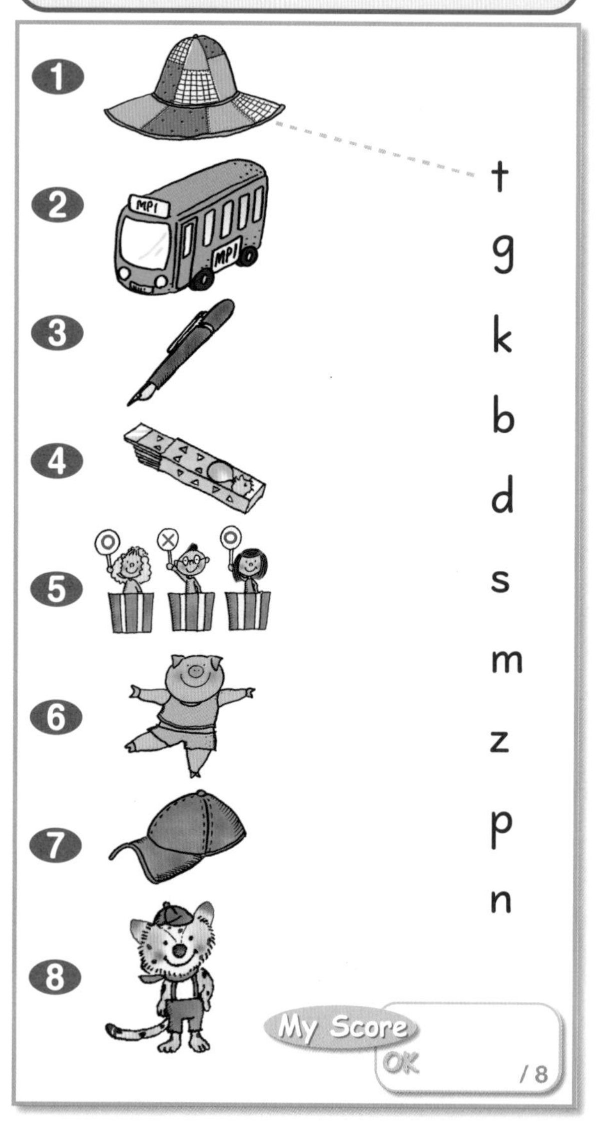

❷ Word Making
（はじめと終わりの文字で単語づくり）
Listen and write the initial and final letters.
（単語のはじめと終わりの文字の音を聞いて書こう。）
6

Game Time!

Pass the Sound（文字の音送り）
Pass the sound in your line. The last person writes the letter.
チームに分かれて文字の音送りリレーをしよう。
最後の人は文字を書こう。

b - v / r - l / m - n

Original Jingle（自分でジングルづくり）
教室の物でジングルをつくろう。

W says w, w
T says . . .

3. Short Vowels

▶（5つの短母音）

意味と音を結びつけておこう。
フォニックスの勉強が楽になるよ。

Vocabulary （単語） 7

❶ Listen and memorize the keywords.
（単語を聞いて覚えよう。）

❷ Point to the pictures and say the words.
（言いながら絵を指さそう。単語を言おう。）

1

2

3
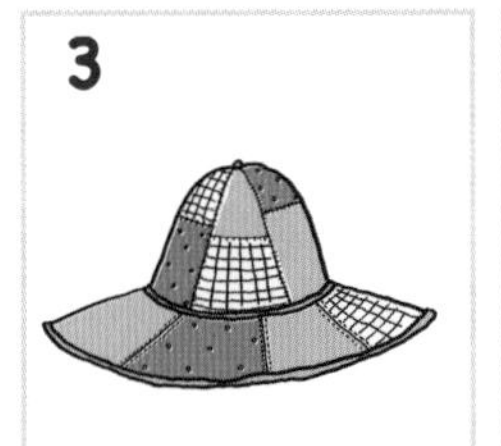

4

5

6

7

8

9

10

11

12

13

14

15
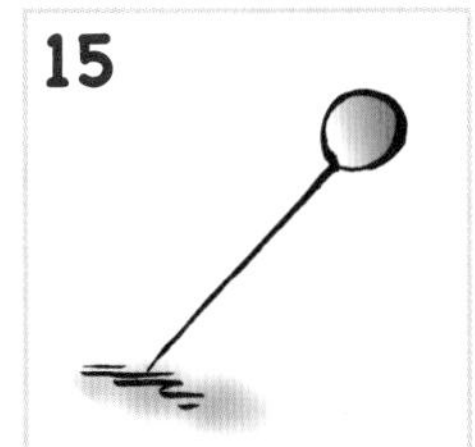

16
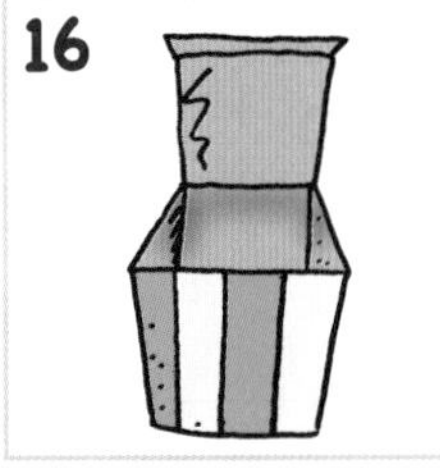

17

18

19

20

21

22

23
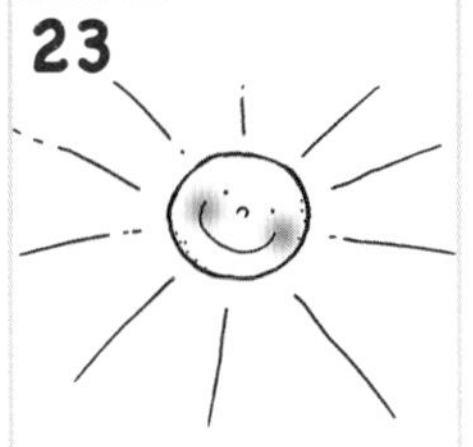

24

25

1 bag	2 cat	3 hat	4 man	5 jam
6 pen	7 men	8 ten	9 bed	10 red
11 pig	12 big	13 sit	14 six	15 pin
16 box	17 hot	18 stop	19 mom	20 top
21 cup	22 run	23 sun	24 bus	25 cut

3. Short Vowels

▶（5 つの短母音）

❶ Rules 1, 5, 9, 15, 21 🔊 8

（音声と動画でルールを知ろう。）

1 文字が 1 音をあらわし、

フォニックスアルファベットの音読みをする母音。

ルールの話
の動画

英語と日本語の母音は音が大きく違う。
マスターすると発音が英語らしくなる。
この 5 文字は母音字。母音は子音と子音をつないで単語をつくる。

❷ Phonics Jingle 🔊 9

（ラップでルールを練習しよう。）

1
a
口を横に開いて、
あごを下げて

5
e
口を横に開いて、
指 2 本、にっこり

❸ Adding Sounds: Clap and say the sounds with rhythm.

（音のたし算：リズムに合わせて手をたたこう。）

Say the sounds.（音を1つずつ言おう。）

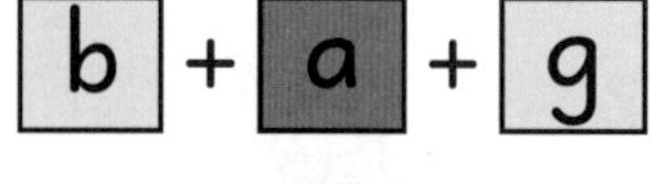

Add the sounds.（音をつなげて言おう。）

b a g

Say the word.（単語を言おう。）

bag

pen

❹ Read the word list on p. 7.（7 ページの単語を読もう。）

❺ Listen and circle the vowel letters.（音声を聞いて、正しい文字を選ぼう。）

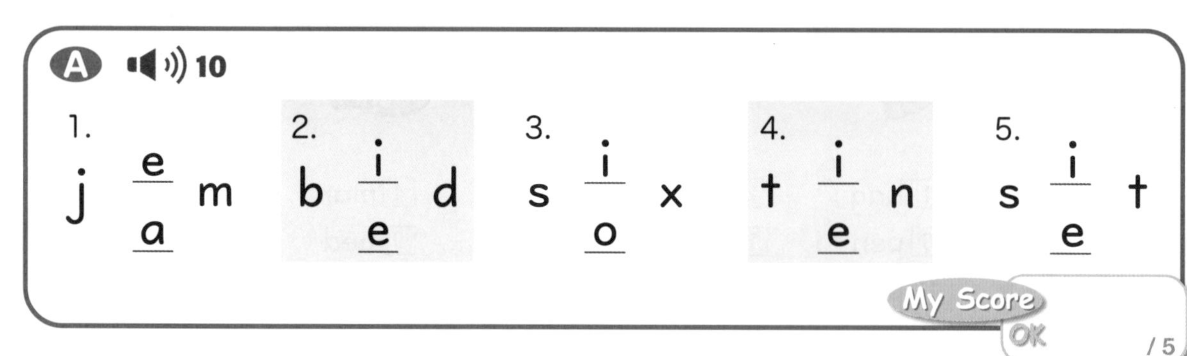

A 🔊 10
1. j e/a m
2. b i/e d
3. s i/o x
4. t i/e n
5. s i/e t
My Score
OK
/ 5

母音の役目は
子音と子音をつなぐ
接着剤。

口を横に開いて、
指 1 本、すまし顔

口をたてに開いて、
指 3 本、大きく

あごを上げて、
上を向いてびっくりして

p + i + g

p i g

pig

b + o + x

b o x

box

c + u + p

c u p

cup

B 11

1. b (e / i) g
2. r (a / u) n
3. h (a / o) t
4. m (u / o) p
5. h (a / u) t

My Score OK / 5

❶ One Finger, Two Fingers （指 1 本、指 2 本?）

Listen to the words. If you think it is No. 1, hold up one finger. If it is No. 2, hold up two fingers. Write 1 or 2 for the final quiz.
（単語を聞いて指 1 本か 2 本で答えよう。最後のクイズは 1 か 2 を書こう。）

12

Write the answers of the final quiz.

A	B	C	D	E

My Score
OK /5

もう一度、チャレンジしてもいいよ。

A	B	C	D	E

My Score
OK /5

❷ Speed Reading （早読み）

Quickly read the words aloud. Clap your hands each time after reading 3 words.
（3つ毎に手をたたいて、単語を早く大きな声で言おう。）

13

sad	not
bad	pot
dad	hot

wit	red
sit	bed
hit	Ted

top	run
hop	sun
pop	fun

似た者同士のファミリー語で
読む練習をしよう。

Game Time!

The Shiritori Game (しりとりゲーム)

Write the words in the boxes and circle the correct pictures.

しりとりをして単語を書こう。合う絵に○をつけよう。

Start

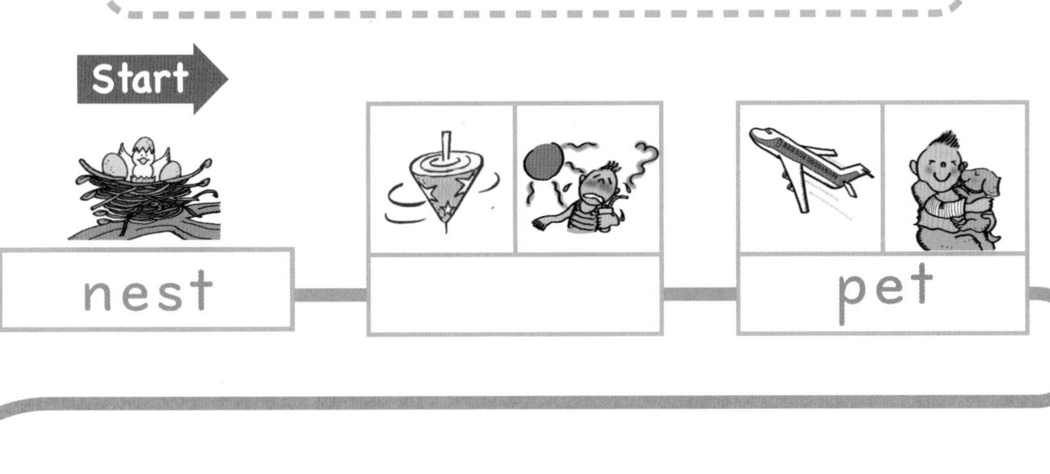

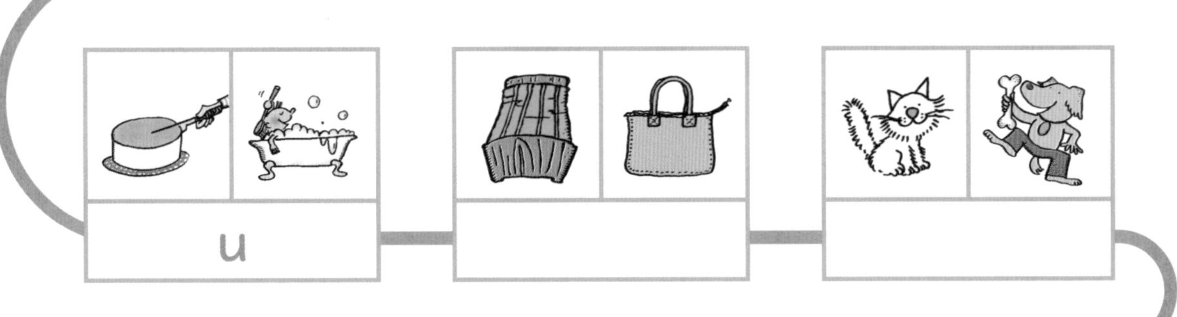

Goal

Wrap-up まとめと練習

Check the boxes after reading the words.
単語が読めたらチェックしよう。

Review ワークブックに出てきた単語
Challenge 1 / Challenge 2 読めるかどうか、チャレンジしてみる語句

Review

1	bad	11	dad	21	map	31	pin	41	Ted
2	bag	12	dog	22	men	32	pop	42	ten
3	bed	13	fun	23	mom	33	pot	43	tent
4	big	14	gum	24	mop	34	red	44	top
5	box	15	hat	25	nest	35	run	45	tub
6	bug	16	hit	26	net	36	sad	46	wit
7	bus	17	hop	27	not	37	sit		
8	cat	18	hot	28	pen	38	six		
9	cup	19	jam	29	pet	39	stop		
10	cut	20	man	30	pig	40	sun		

Challenge 1

1	bat	7	dig	13	gun	19	leg	25	set
2	bun	8	dot	14	ham	20	log	26	tag
3	but	9	fan	15	hen	21	mix	27	tap
4	can	10	fig	16	hug	22	mug	28	vet
5	cap	11	fox	17	jet	23	nut	29	wet
6	cub	12	get	18	jog	24	pan	30	win

Challenge 2

1	bag–bug	4	cat–cut	7	pen–pan	10	sun–sin
2	big–bag	5	man–men	8	pin–pan	11	ten–tan
3	cap–cup	6	mop–map	9	stop–step	12	top–tap

4. Silent E

▶（Eのついた母音）

カタカナで知っている単語もあるね。
音の違いに注意しよう。

Vocabulary （単語） 14

❶ Listen and memorize the keywords.
（単語を聞いて覚えよう。）

❷ Point to the pictures and say the words.
（言いながら絵を指さそう。単語を言おう。）

1

2
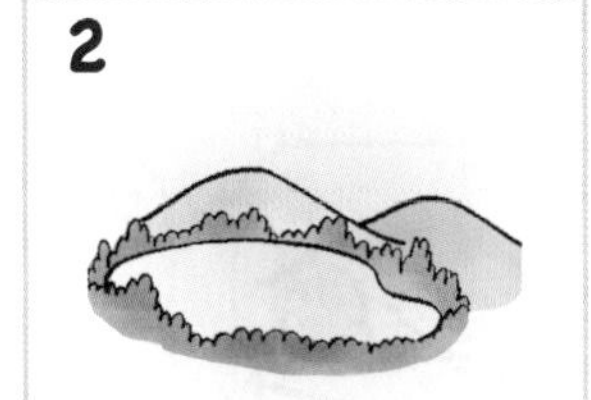

3
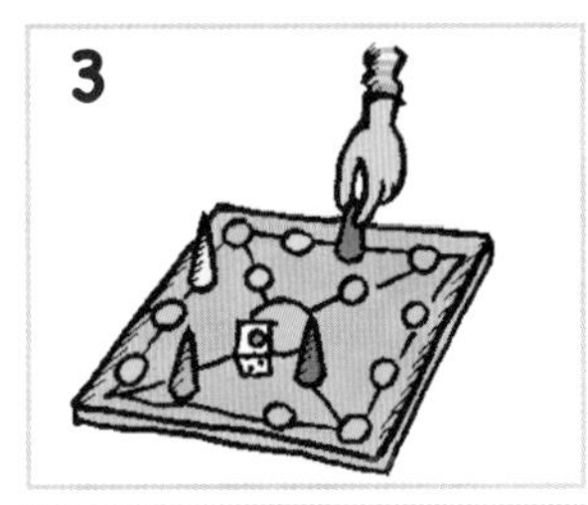

4

5

6

7

8

9

10

11

12

13

14

15

16

17
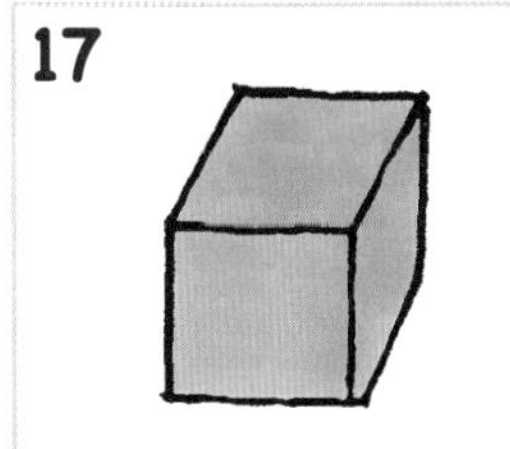

18

19

20

1 cake	2 lake	3 game	4 name
5 Pete	6 Eve	7 he	8 we
9 five	10 nine	11 time	12 bike
13 rose	14 nose	15 home	16 pole
17 cube	18 tube	19 cute	20 June

4. Silent E

▶（E のついた母音）

❶ Rules 27 - 31 15

（音声と動画でルールを知ろう。）
最初の文字を名前読みし、2 番目の母音字は読まないグループで e で終わるもの。

ルールの話
の動画

❷ Phonics Jingle 16

（ラップでルールを練習しよう。）

❸ Adding Sounds: Clap and say the sounds with rhythm.

（音のたし算：リズムに合わせて手をたたこう。）

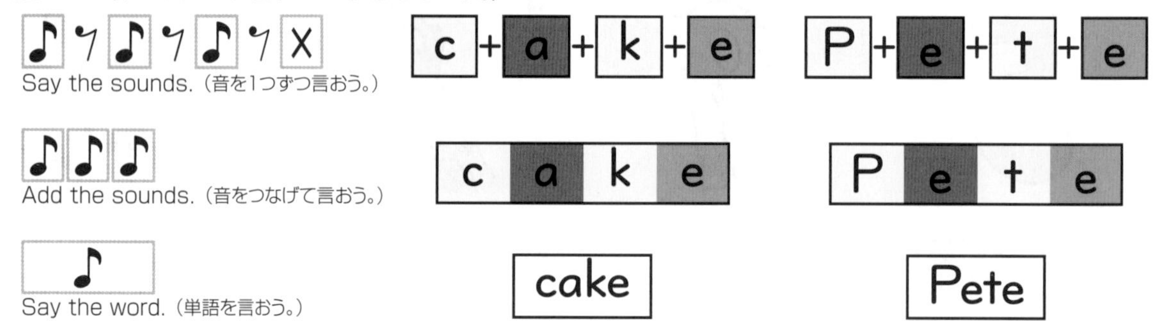

❹ Read the word list on p. 13.（13 ページの単語を読もう。）

❺ Listen and fill in the blanks.（音声を聞いて、空所に文字を入れよう。）

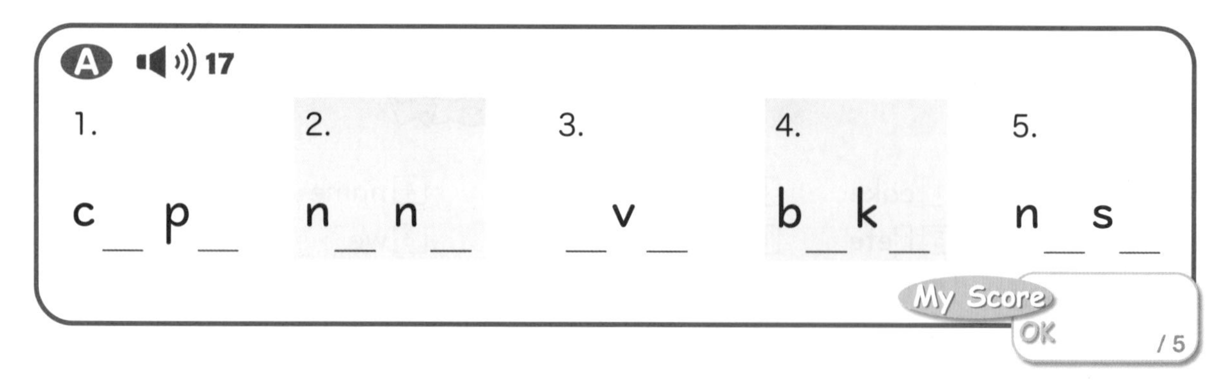

単語のしっぽについたSilent Eは前の母音にマジックをかけて名前読みにする。でも自分はサイレントで音を出さない。

（注）名前読み＝アルファベットの「名前」通りに読む。
音（おと）読み＝フォニックスアルファベットの「音」通りに読む。

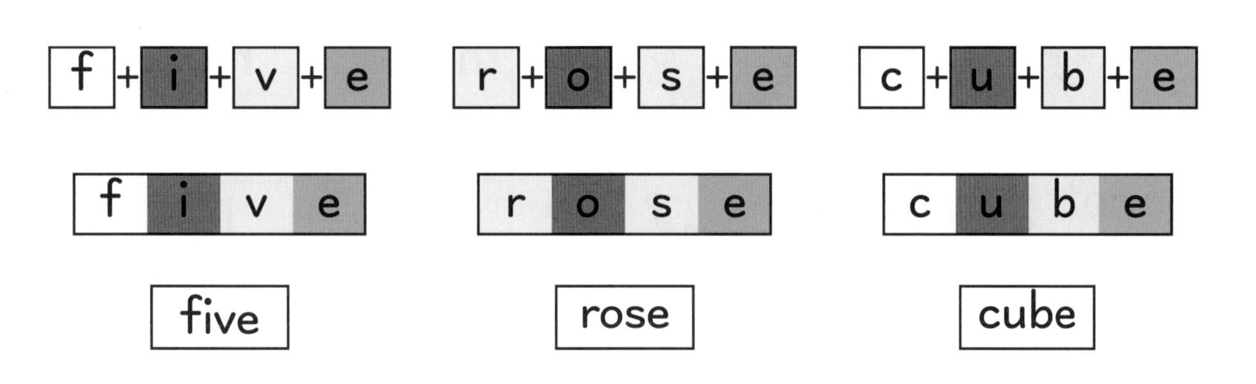

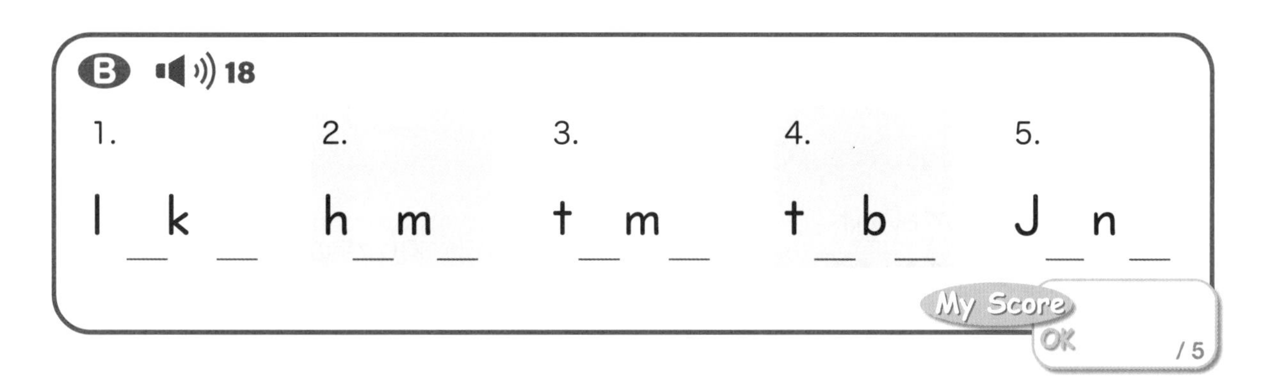

❶ One Finger, Two Fingers（指 1 本、指 2 本?）

Listen to the words. If you think it is No. 1, hold up one finger. If it is No. 2, hold up two fingers. Write 1 or 2 for the final quiz.
（単語を聞いて指 1 本か 2 本で答えよう。最後のクイズは 1 か 2 を書こう。）

19

	1.	2.
A	hat	hate
B	pet	Pete
C	cut	cute
D	not	note
E	cap	cape

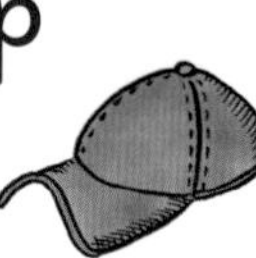

Write the answers of the final quiz.

A	B	C	D	E

My Score
OK /5

もう一度、チャレンジしてもいいよ。

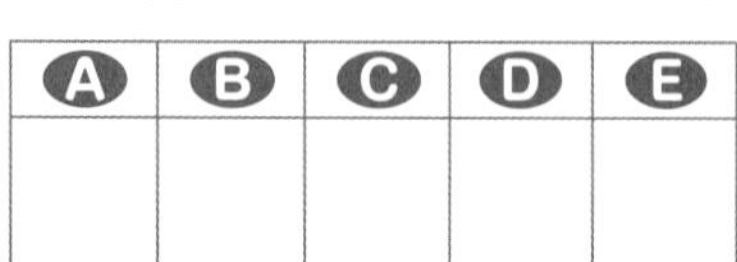

A	B	C	D	E

❷ Speed Reading（早読み）

Quickly read the words aloud.
（単語を早く大きな声で言おう。）

13

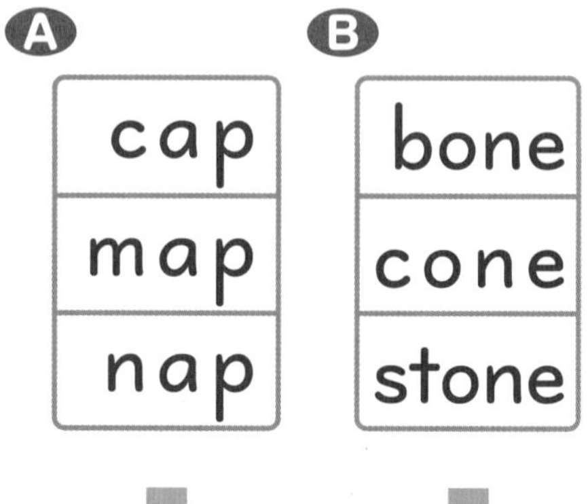

A	B
cap	bone
map	cone
nap	stone

A	B
make	not
cake	hot
take	lot

A	B
nine	nose
fine	rose
mine	close

同じ文字のところに
下線を引いてみよう。

❸ Matching with Pictures（絵・文字合わせ）

Read the words. Connect the pictures and words with lines. Fold the page on the broken line.
（単語を読んで、合う絵と結ぼう。点線で谷折りしよう。）
18ページの問題も続けてやろう。

cap •	• 1
mat •	• 2
Pet •	• 3
pin •	• 4
Tim •	• 5
hop •	• 6
not •	• 7
cut •	• 8

谷折り

❹ Scrambled Letters

（単語探し）
Find and write the words.
（バラバラ文字を単語にしよう。）

1. c a e k ＿ ＿ ＿ ＿
2. e u t b ＿ ＿ ＿ ＿
3. e w ＿ ＿
4. v i f e ＿ ＿ ＿ ＿
5. a e m n ＿ ＿ ＿ ＿
6. o e h m ＿ ＿ ＿ ＿
7. l k e a ＿ ＿ ＿ ＿
8. u J e n ＿ ＿ ＿ ＿

Hints

My Score OK /8

Matching with Pictures
（絵・文字合わせ）

Fold the page on the broken line and read the new words. Connect the pictures and words with lines.
（線で山折りして単語を読もう。合う絵と結ぼう。）

e •

e •

e •

e •

e •

e •

e •

e •

❶ •

❷ •

❸ •

❹ •

❺ •

❻ •

❼ •

❽ •

山折り

❺ Write the answers.
（単語を書こう。）

Look at the pictures on the left and write the words.
（左の絵を見て下線に単語を書こう。）

❶ ______ ❺ ______

❷ ______ ❻ ______

❸ ______ ❼ ______

❹ ______ ❽ ______

My Score OK /8

Game Time!

Listen and Write the Words!

リーダーが単語を選んで、シャウト!
聞こえた単語を書こう。

cute!

cut!

❶ ______ ❷ ______

❸ ______ ❹ ______

Wrap-up まとめと練習

Check the boxes after reading the words.
単語が読めたらチェックしよう。

Review ワークブックに出てきた単語
Challenge 1 / Challenge 2 読めるかどうか、チャレンジしてみる語句・文

Review

1	☐	bike	11	☐	five	21	☐	mat	31	☐	pole	41	☐	hat–hate
2	☐	bone	12	☐	game	22	☐	mate	32	☐	rose	42	☐	hop–hope
3	☐	cake	13	☐	hate	23	☐	mine	33	☐	stone	43	☐	mat–mate
4	☐	cape	14	☐	he	24	☐	name	34	☐	take	44	☐	not–note
5	☐	close	15	☐	home	25	☐	nap	35	☐	Tim	45	☐	pet–Pete
6	☐	cone	16	☐	hope	26	☐	nine	36	☐	time	46	☐	pin–pine
7	☐	cube	17	☐	June	27	☐	nose	37	☐	tube	47	☐	Tim–time
8	☐	cute	18	☐	lake	28	☐	note	38	☐	we			
9	☐	Eve	19	☐	lot	29	☐	Pete	39	☐	cap–cape			
10	☐	fine	20	☐	make	30	☐	pine	40	☐	cut–cute			

Challenge 1

1	☐	ate	7	☐	gate	13	☐	line	19	☐	rope	25	☐	can–cane
2	☐	base	8	☐	hide	14	☐	made	20	☐	safe	26	☐	pal–pale
3	☐	brave	9	☐	hole	15	☐	nice	21	☐	stole	27	☐	sit–site
4	☐	came	10	☐	late	16	☐	rice	22	☐	wave	28	☐	tap–tape
5	☐	dive	11	☐	life	17	☐	ride	23	☐	wide	29	☐	tub–tube
6	☐	face	12	☐	like	18	☐	role	24	☐	write	30	☐	win–wine

Challenge 2

1	☐	a big nose	4	☐	game time	7	☐	He can go home.
2	☐	a cute pig	5	☐	Bob can skate.	8	☐	Meg can ride a bike.
3	☐	brave men	6	☐	Eve can make a cute cape.			

65のルール以外で、英語を読む時に役立つ読み方を紹介するよ！

1 Soft c Soft g ソフトcとソフトg

Sの音

cent/city
セント 都市

cの後に e が来る時、cはSの音。

jの音

gentle/giant
優しい 巨人

gの後に i がくる時、gはjの音。

1. cent セント 2. cement セメント 3. centimeter センチメートル
4. city 都市 5. cicada セミ 6. Cinderella シンデレラ

7. gentle 優しい 8. gel ジェル 9. gem 宝石 10. gelatin ゼラチン
11. giant 巨人 12. ginger ショウガ

Let's Read!
□cicada □gelatin □ginger □cement □cent □gem
□Cinderella □gel □centimeter □giant □gentle □city

2 母音が1つで最後につく

名前読み

no
いいえ

単語の中に母音が1つで、
その母音で終わるものは
名前読み。

1. no いいえ 2. go 行く 3. so だから 4. hi やあ
5. me 私に 6. be ～である

Let's Read!
□hi □no □be □me □so □go

3 その他の名前読みする母音

名前読み

old
古い

名前読み

find
見つける

ld と nd の前の母音は名前読み。

1. old 古い 2. cold 寒い 3. gold 金 4. told 語った
5. child こども 6. mild 温和な 7. wild 野生の

8. find 見つける 9. kind 親切な 10. mind 心 11. binder バインダー

Let's Read!
□kind □mild □mind □cold □child □told □binder
□old □gold □find □wild

5. Polite Vowels

▶ (礼儀正しい母音)

ルールを知る前にまず単語を確認しよう。

Vocabulary (単語) 🔊 20

❶ **Listen and memorize the keywords.**
(単語を聞いて覚えよう。)

❷ **Point to the pictures and say the words.**
(言いながら絵を指さそう。単語を言おう。)

1

2

3

4

5

6

7

8

9

10

11

12

13

14

15

16

17

18

19

20

1 rain	2 wait	3 May	4 play
5 day	6 tea	7 read	8 eat
9 week	10 sleep	11 pie	12 tie
13 boat	14 road	15 snow	16 window
17 blue	18 glue	19 fruit	20 juice

5. Polite Vowels

▶（礼儀正しい母音）

❶ Rules 32-40 🔊 21

（音声と動画でルールを知ろう。）
母音が２つ並んでいて前の母音は名前読み、後ろは読まないグループ。

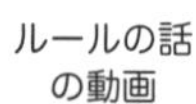

❷ Phonics Jingle 🔊 22

（ラップでルールを練習しよう。）

33
ay
SMTWTFS
5
前の母音が名前読み

❸ Adding Sounds

（音のたし算）

Add the sounds.（音をつなげて言おう。）

Say the word.（単語を言おう。）

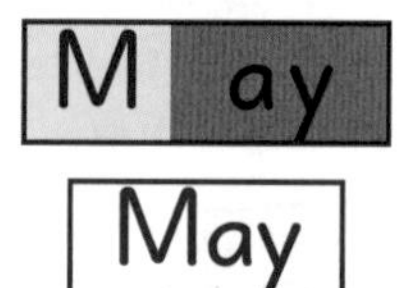

❹ Read the word list on p. 21.

（21 ページの単語を読もう。）

❺ Listen and circle the vowel letters.

（音声を聞いて、正しいルールを選ぼう。）

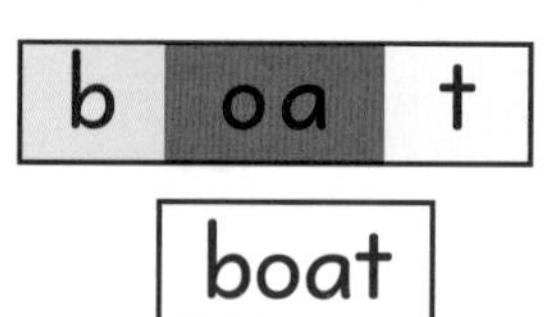

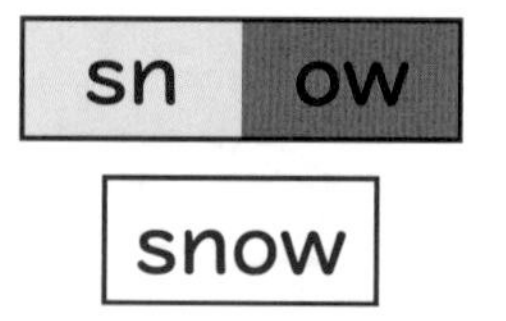

Ⓐ 🔊 23

1. (ai • ie)
2. (ie • ea)
3. (oa • ui)
4. (ea • ui)
5. (ee • ai)

My Score OK / 5

母音字が２つ並んで歩いていました。最初の母音は元気よく自分の名前を言い、後ろの母音は礼儀正しくて静かについていきました。

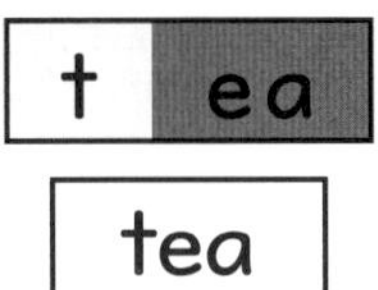

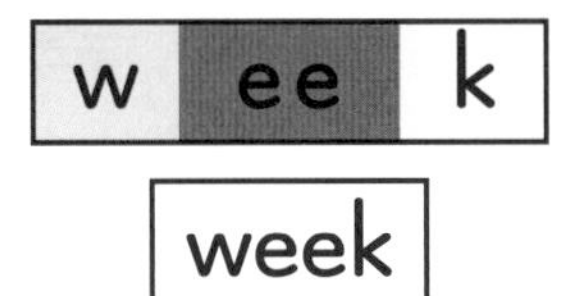

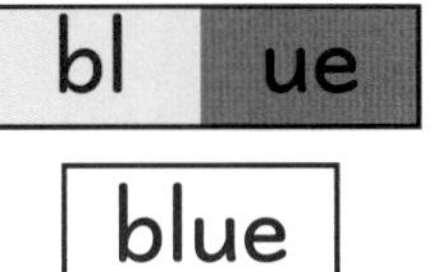

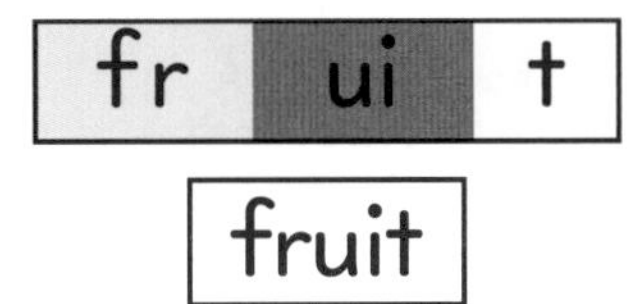

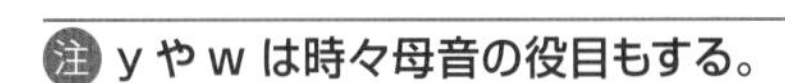

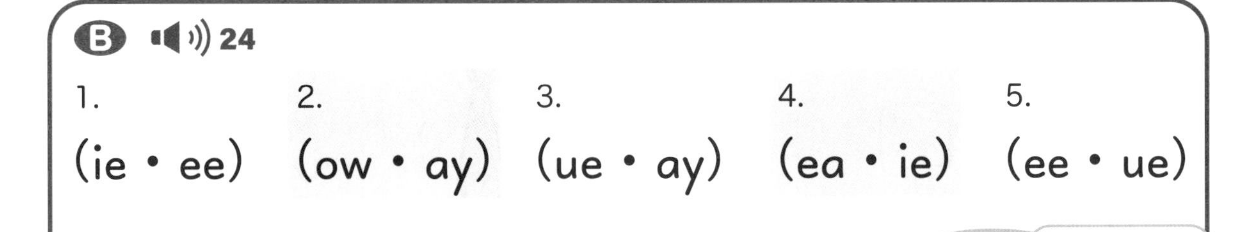

B 24
1. (ie • ee)
2. (ow • ay)
3. (ue • ay)
4. (ea • ie)
5. (ee • ue)
My Score
OK
/ 5

❶ Find the rules（ルール探し）

Look at the 3 symbols for 3 vowel rules.
Draw the correct symbol on each word.
（3 種類の母音のルールを見つけて印をつけよう。）

❷ Matching with Pictures（絵・文字合わせ）

Match the words with the pictures. Write the correct alphabet letters in the boxes.
（左の単語を声を出して読み、絵を右から選び、その記号を書こう。）

read
Polite Vowels
礼儀正しい母音

red
Short Vowels
５つの短母音

lake
Silent E
Eのついた母音

❶	read	f
❷	day	
❸	snow	
❹	fruit	
❺	men	
❻	tie	
❼	five	
❽	wait	
❾	sleep	
❿	jam	
⓫	tea	
⓬	June	

a

b

c

d

e 5

f

g
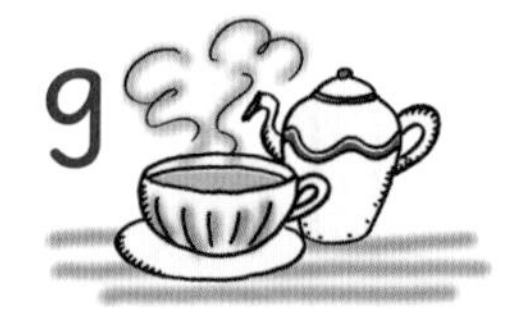

h

i 6月

j

k

l

My Score OK / 12

❸ Speed Reading（早読み）

Quickly read the words aloud.
（単語を早く大きな声で言おう。）

🔊 13

see	pie
tree	tie
free	die
blue	day
glue	say
Sue	May
boat	tea
coat	pea
goat	sea

Game Time!

Odd One Out（絵を見て違うルールの絵に○をつけよう。）

A

1. 

2. 

3. 

B

1. 

2. 

3. 

C

1. 

2. 

3. 

❹ Grouping（仲間探し）

Say and write the words from the pictures.
（絵を見て単語を言おう。単語を書こう。）

ie

パイはネクタイをして食べよう。

____

____

ee

1週間寝てくらす。

____

____

ea

読みながら食べるな！

____

____

ai

雨が止むまで待とう。

____

____

ow

窓に雪がつもった。

____

____

ui

フルーツジュース1本。

____

____

Wrap-up まとめと練習

Check the boxes after reading the words.
単語が読めたらチェックしよう。

Review ワークブックに出てきた単語
Challenge 1 / Challenge 2 読めるかどうか、チャレンジしてみる語句・文

Review

1	☐ blue	7	☐ free	13	☐ pea	19	☐ say	25	☐ suit
2	☐ boat	8	☐ fruit	14	☐ pie	20	☐ sea	26	☐ tea
3	☐ coat	9	☐ glue	15	☐ play	21	☐ see	27	☐ tie
4	☐ day	10	☐ goat	16	☐ rain	22	☐ sleep	28	☐ wait
5	☐ die	11	☐ juice	17	☐ read	23	☐ snow	29	☐ week
6	☐ eat	12	☐ May	18	☐ road	24	☐ Sue	30	☐ window

Challenge 1

1	☐ bean	7	☐ e-mail	13	☐ meet	19	☐ scream	25	☐ toast
2	☐ beef	8	☐ feet	14	☐ nail	20	☐ seat	26	☐ way
3	☐ clean	9	☐ goal	15	☐ pain	21	☐ speak	27	☐ weak
4	☐ cream	10	☐ gray	16	☐ rainbow	22	☐ sweet	28	☐ yellow
5	☐ deep	11	☐ lie	17	☐ rainy	23	☐ tail		
6	☐ dream	12	☐ meat	18	☐ row	24	☐ team		

Challenge 2

1	☐ a big yellow snail	10	☐ snow on the window
2	☐ a blue snake	11	☐ the deep sea
3	☐ a coat on the boat	12	☐ toast and lemon juice
4	☐ a green tree	13	☐ Do you like roast beef?
5	☐ a hot tea cup	14	☐ He has a blue raincoat.
6	☐ a yellow glue	15	☐ I have one tea cup.
7	☐ green tea ice cream	16	☐ I like your gray coat.
8	☐ meat pie	17	☐ I play a game.
9	☐ rain on the train	18	☐ Let’s eat fruit pie.

65 のルール以外で、英語を読む時に役立つ読み方を紹介するよ！

4 音なし子音

読まないよ　単語の中に文字はあるけれど、赤い子音字は読まない。

knife ナイフ　kn = n の音

1. knife ナイフ　2. know 知っている　3. knee ひざ

write 書く　wr = r の音

4. write 書く　5. wrap つつむ　6. wrist 手首

high 高い　igh = i の音（名前読み）

7. high 高い　8. night 夜　9. light 明かり

bridge 橋　dge = j の音

10. bridge 橋　11. judge 審判　12. dodgeball ドッヂボール

Let's Read!

□night □wrist □judge □know □write □dodgeball
□light □wrap □knife □bridge □high □knee

Sight Word List

（見て覚える単語）

よく登場するがルールに当てはまらない単語は見て覚えよう。

a	are	as	is	do
does	don't	I	of	to
the	you	yours	have	has
any	busy	every	from	many
over	here	there	they	their
who	whose	where	one	give

65 のルール以外で、英語を読む時に役立つ読み方を紹介するよ！

5 i の名前読みする y

i の名前読み

fly
飛ぶ

単語の中で y が唯一の母音の時、y は i の名前読み。

1. fly 飛ぶ　2. cry 泣く　3. dry 乾いた　4. sky 空
5. my 私の　6. by ～のそばに / ～によって

Let's Read! □sky □my □cry □by □fly □dry

Interview

Ask your teachers and friends these questions.
先生や友達に質問してみよう。

Questions	name		
① Do you have a pet?	Yes/No	Yes/No	Yes/No
② Do you have a bike?	Yes/No	Yes/No	Yes/No
③ Do you have a boat?	Yes/No	Yes/No	Yes/No
④ Do you have a red coat?	Yes/No	Yes/No	Yes/No
⑤ Do you have a blue tie?	Yes/No	Yes/No	Yes/No
⑥ Do you like fruit juice?	Yes/No	Yes/No	Yes/No
⑦ Do you like roast beef?	Yes/No	Yes/No	Yes/No
⑧ Do you like celery?	Yes/No	Yes/No	Yes/No
⑨ Do you like dodgeball?	Yes/No	Yes/No	Yes/No
⑩ Do you like green tea ice cream?	Yes/No	Yes/No	Yes/No

6. Consonant Digraphs

（2文字子音）

Vocabulary （単語） 25

❶ **Listen and memorize the keywords.**
（単語を聞いて覚えよう。）

❷ **Point to the pictures and say the words.**
（言いながら絵を指さそう。単語を言おう。）

1 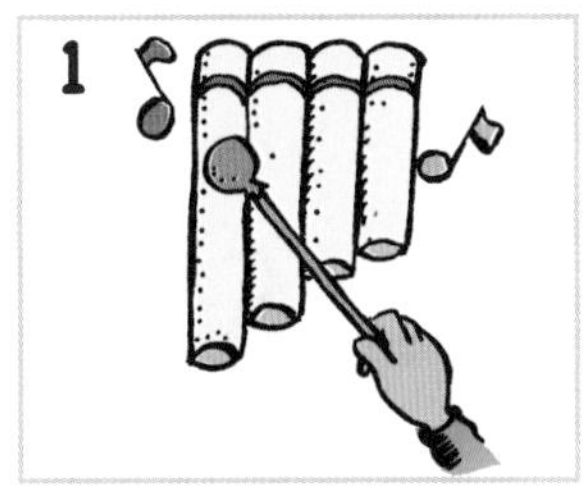

2 

3 

4 

5 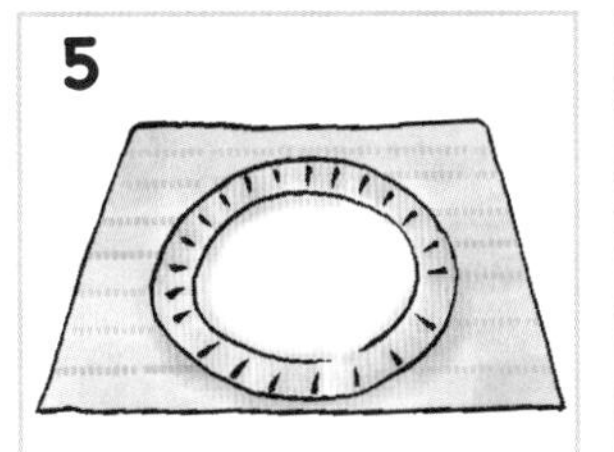

6 

7 

8 

9 

10 

11 

12 

13 

14 

15 

16 

17 

18 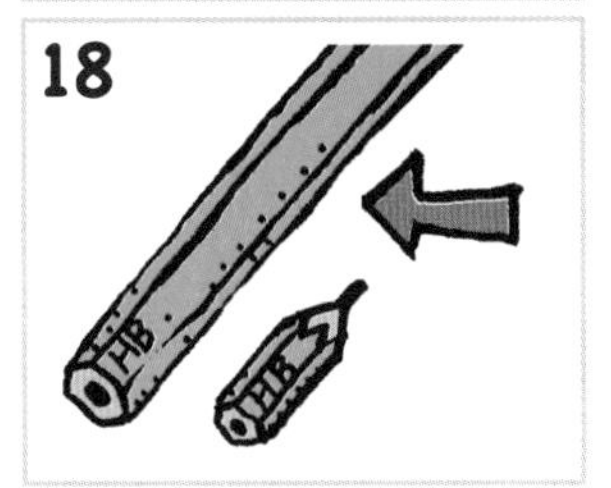

19 

20 

1 chime	2 teach	3 lunch	4 ship
5 dish	6 fish	7 think	8 math
9 this	10 that	11 these	12 those
13 white	14 whale	15 phone	16 elephant
17 sing	18 long	19 back	20 rock

6. Consonant Digraphs ▶（2文字子音）

❶ Rules 41-48 🔊 26

（音声と動画でルールを知ろう。）
2つの子音字が新しい1音をつくるルール。
くっつきのhが注意信号文字。

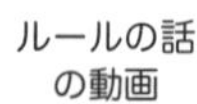

❷ Phonics Jingle 🔊 27

（ラップでルールを練習しよう。）

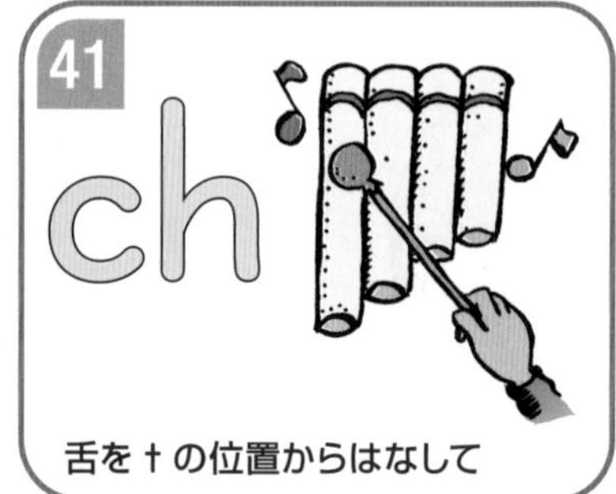

41
ch
舌をｔの位置からはなして

42
sh
口をつき出し息だけで

❸ Break down the word.

（単語の音を1音ごとに分けよう。）

Say the word.
（単語を言おう。）

Break into sounds.
（1音ごとに分けて□に書こう。）

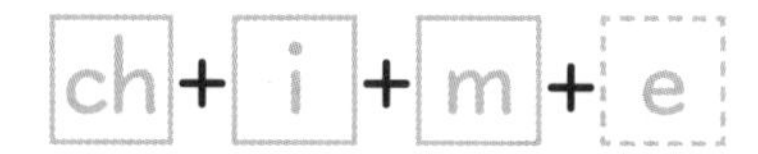

How many letters?
How many sounds?

45
th
舌をはさんで息だけで

46
th
舌をはさんで声出して

❹ Read the word list on p. 29.

（29ページの単語を読もう。）

❺ Listen and fill in the blanks.

（音声を聞いて、空所に文字を入れよう。）

A 🔊 28

1. tea _ _
2. fi _ _
3. ele _ _ ant
4. lun _ _
5. di _ _

My Score OK /5

c と h がくっついて声を出したら
新しい音になる。

f と同じ、下くちびるをかんで

くちびるつき出し、 胸の奥から

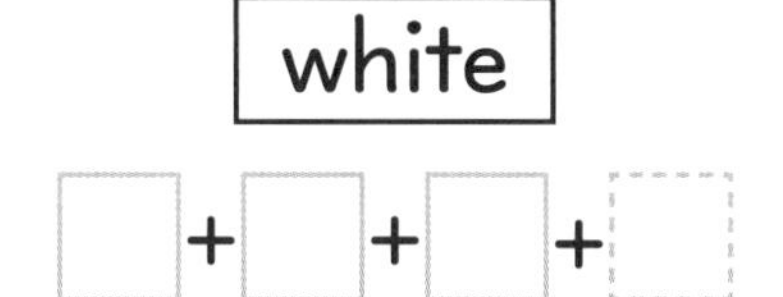

この2つは単語の最初にはこない。

k と同じ音

鼻にぬかして1つの音

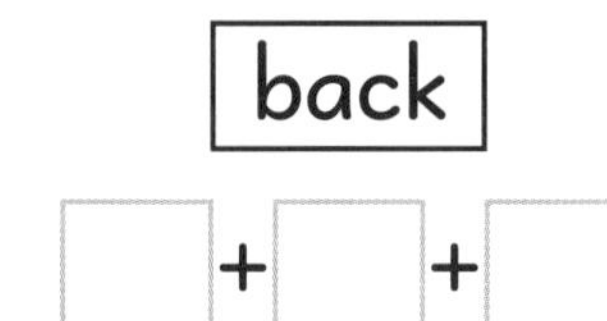

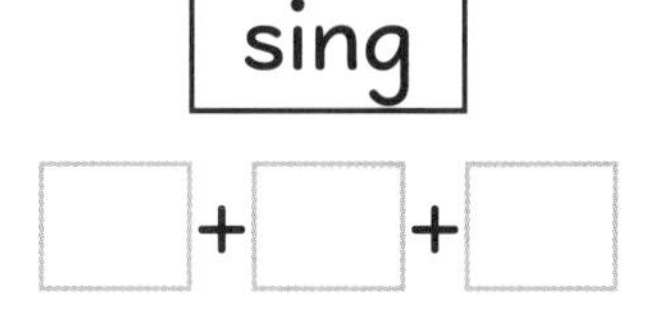

B 29

1. ba__ __
2. __ __at
3. __ __ale
4. lo__ __
5. ro__ __

My Score OK / 5

❶ One Finger, Two Fingers（指1本、指2本?）

Listen to the words. If you think it is No. 1, hold up one finger. If it is No. 2, hold up two fingers. Write 1 or 2 for the final quiz.
（単語を聞いて指1本か2本で答えよう。最後のクイズは1か2を書こう。）

30

A	B	C	D	E

もう一度、チャレンジしてもいいよ。

A	B	C	D	E

❷ Speed Reading（早読み）

Clap your hands each time after reading 3 words.
（3つ毎に手をたたいて読もう。）

13

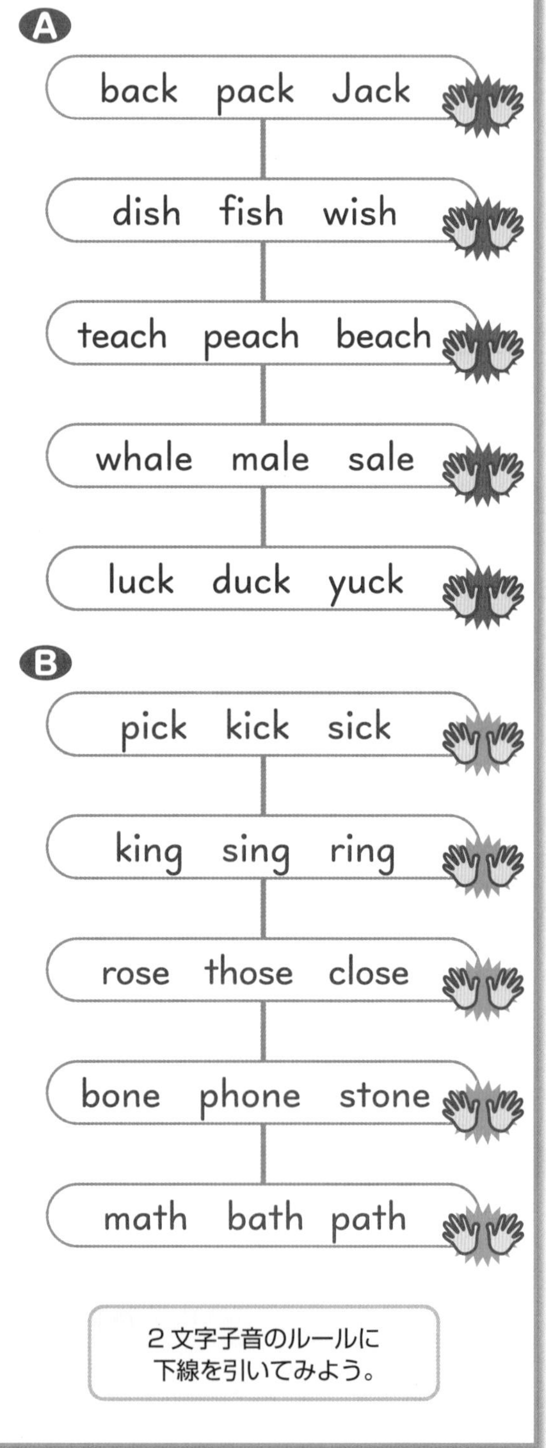

A
back pack Jack
dish fish wish
teach peach beach
whale male sale
luck duck yuck
B
pick kick sick
king sing ring
rose those close
bone phone stone
math bath path
2文字子音のルールに
下線を引いてみよう。

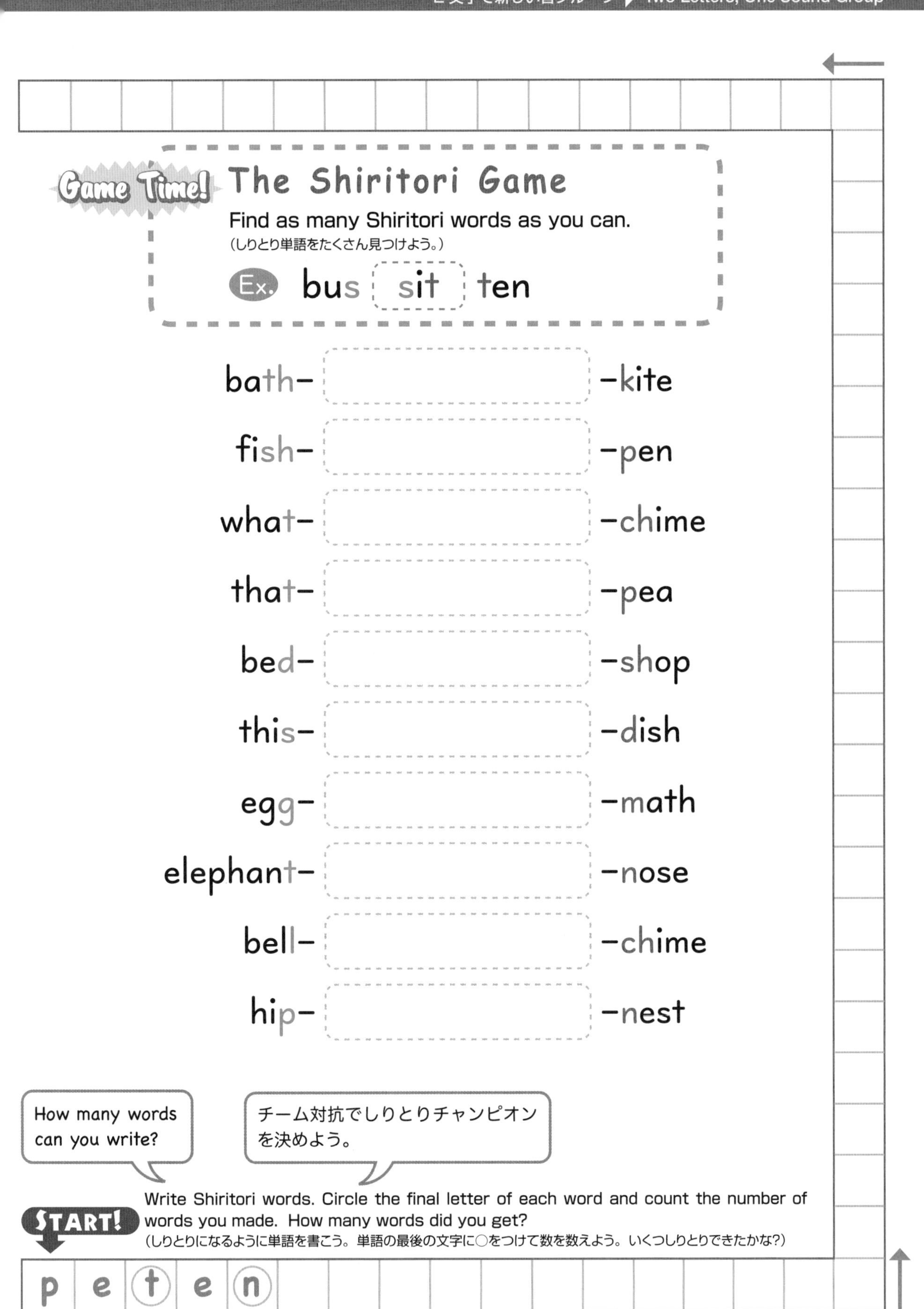

Game Time! The Shiritori Game

Find as many Shiritori words as you can.
（しりとり単語をたくさん見つけよう。）

Ex. bus sit ten

bath- -kite
fish- -pen
what- -chime
that- -pea
bed- -shop
this- -dish
egg- -math
elephant- -nose
bell- -chime
hip- -nest

How many words can you write?
チーム対抗でしりとりチャンピオンを決めよう。
START!
p e t e n

Write Shiritori words. Circle the final letter of each word and count the number of words you made. How many words did you get?
（しりとりになるように単語を書こう。単語の最後の文字に○をつけて数を数えよう。いくつしりとりできたかな?）

Wrap-up まとめと練習

Check the boxes after reading the words.
単語が読めたらチェックしよう。

Review ワークブックに出てきた単語
Challenge 1 / Challenge 2 読めるかどうか、チャレンジしてみる語句・文

Review

1	☐ back	11	☐ Jack	21	☐ path	31	☐ shop	41	☐ those
2	☐ bath	12	☐ kick	22	☐ peach	32	☐ sick	42	☐ whale
3	☐ beach	13	☐ king	23	☐ phone	33	☐ sing	43	☐ what
4	☐ bell	14	☐ kite	24	☐ pick	34	☐ sink	44	☐ white
5	☐ chime	15	☐ long	25	☐ ring	35	☐ teach	45	☐ wish
6	☐ dish	16	☐ luck	26	☐ rock	36	☐ that	46	☐ wrong
7	☐ duck	17	☐ lunch	27	☐ Ron	37	☐ these	47	☐ yuck
8	☐ elephant	18	☐ male	28	☐ sale	38	☐ thick		
9	☐ fish	19	☐ math	29	☐ she	39	☐ think		
10	☐ hip	20	☐ pack	30	☐ ship	40	☐ this		

Challenge 1

1	☐ bench	8	☐ jacket	15	☐ pocket	22	☐ shy	29	☐ thing
2	☐ check	9	☐ lung	16	☐ racket	23	☐ song	30	☐ wash
3	☐ cheese	10	☐ much	17	☐ running	24	☐ teeth	31	☐ wheel
4	☐ China	11	☐ neck	18	☐ sandwich	25	☐ thank	32	☐ when
5	☐ Chinese	12	☐ phonics	19	☐ shake	26	☐ them		
6	☐ dolphin	13	☐ photo	20	☐ shine	27	☐ then		
7	☐ fifth	14	☐ ping-pong	21	☐ show	28	☐ thin		

Challenge 2

1	☐ a cheese sandwich	7	☐ I sing a song.
2	☐ a dolphin show	8	☐ I take a bath.
3	☐ a pet shop	9	☐ Take a chance.
4	☐ chocolate ice cream	10	☐ Thank you so much.
5	☐ ethnic food	11	☐ The ring is in my pocket.
6	☐ He can teach math.	12	☐ We play ping-pong.

7. Vowel Digraphs

（2文字母音）

Vocabulary （単語） 31

❶ Listen and memorize the keywords.
（単語を聞いて覚えよう。）

❷ Point to the pictures and say the words.
（言いながら絵を指さそう。単語を言おう。）

1

2

3

4
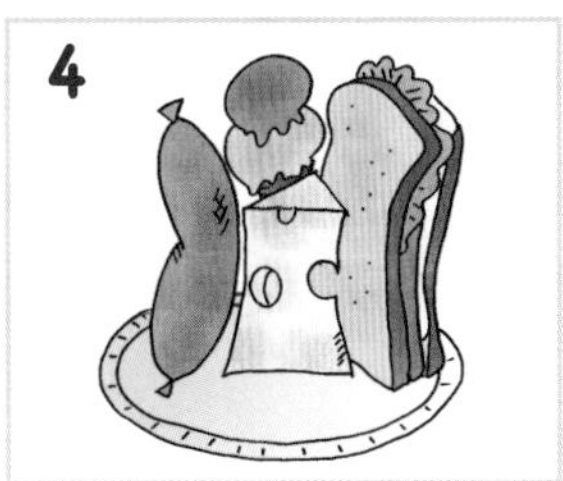

5

6

7

8
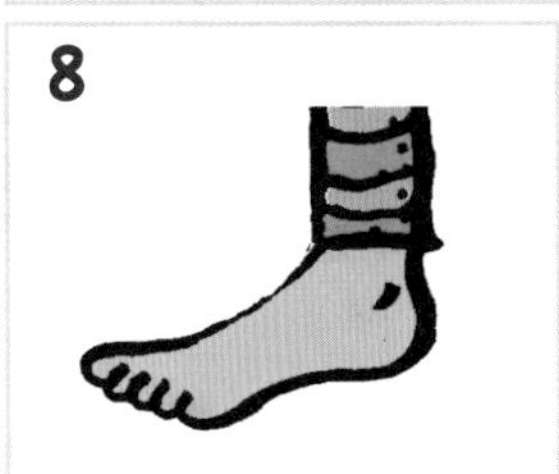

9

10
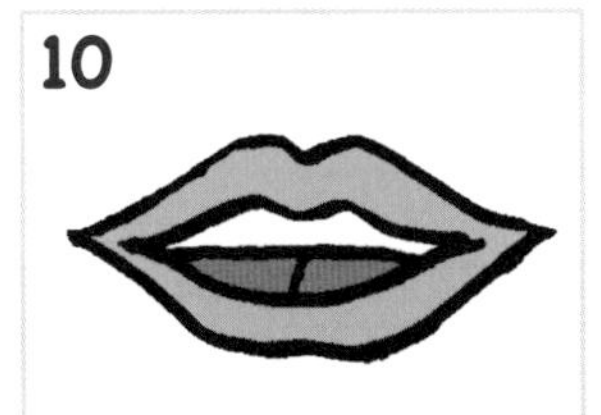

11
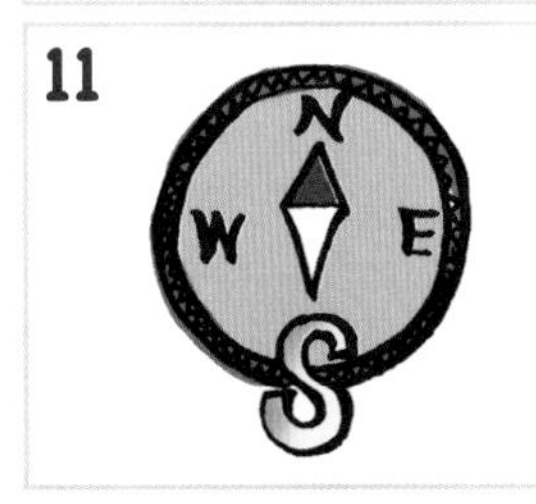

12
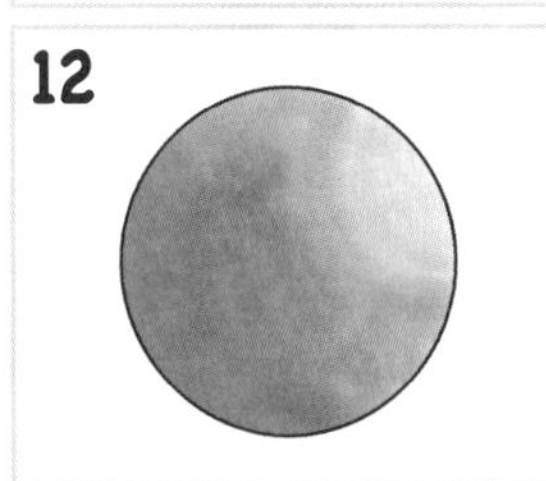

13

14

15

16
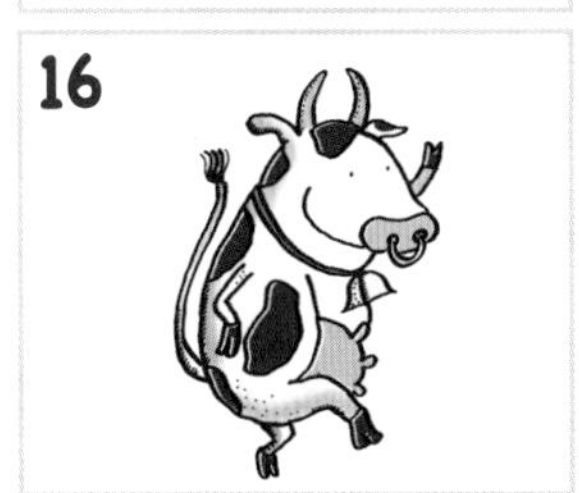

17

18

19

20

1 room	2 noon	3 pool	4 food
5 book	6 cook	7 look	8 foot
9 house	10 mouth	11 south	12 round
13 town	14 down	15 brown	16 cow
17 coin	18 noisy	19 boy	20 enjoy

7. Vowel Digraphs

▶（2 文字母音）

❶ Rules 49- 54 32

（音声と動画でルールを知ろう。）

母音が 2 つ並んで新しい音をつくるルール。

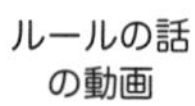

❷ Phonics Jingle 33

（ラップでルールを練習しよう。）

❸ Break down the word.

（単語の音を 1 音ごとに分けよう。）

Say the word.

（単語を言おう。）

Break into sounds.

（1 音ごとに分けて□に書こう。）

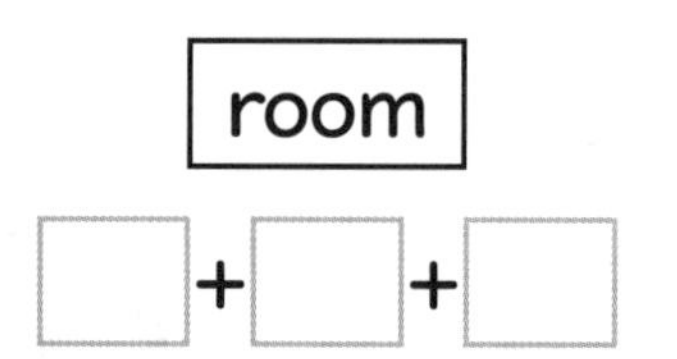

53
oi
はじめを強く、2 つめをそっと

54
oy
はじめを強く、2 つめをそっと

❹ Read the word list on p. 35.

（35 ページの単語を読もう。）

❺ Listen and fill in the blanks.

（音声を聞いて、空所に文字を入れよう。）

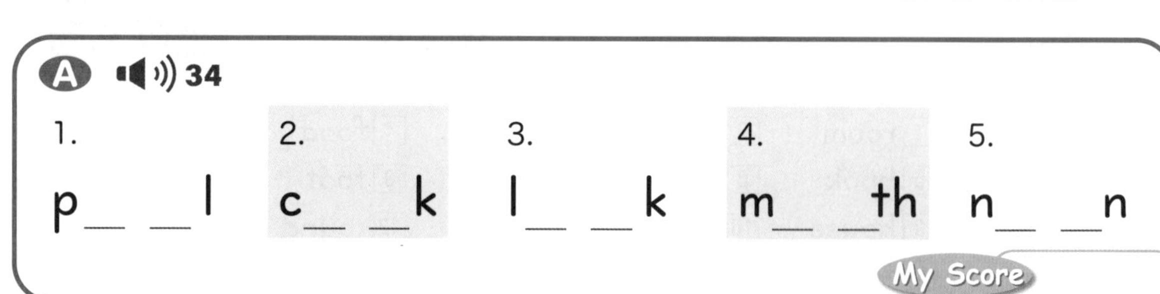

oo はお父さんとお母さん似。
だけど声は違うよ。

51
ou
はじめを強く、２つめをそっと

52
ow
はじめを強く、２つめをそっと

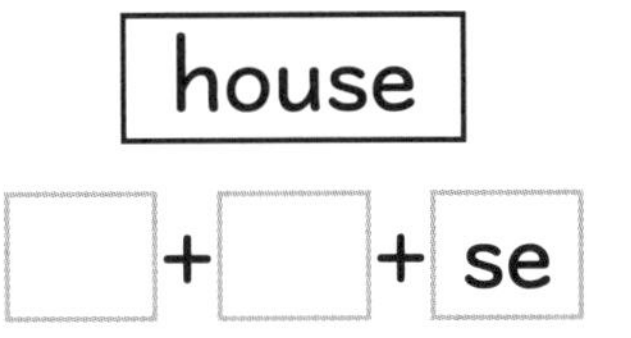

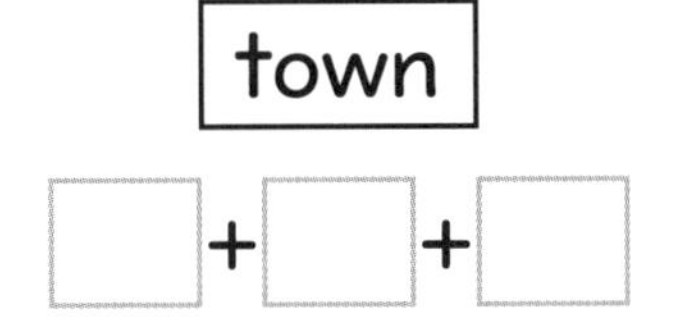

これも知っておくと便利

au			aw		
	August	８月		saw	見た
	sauce	ソース		straw	わら
	Paul	ポール		jaw	あご

口をたてに開けあごを下げ、口の奥から

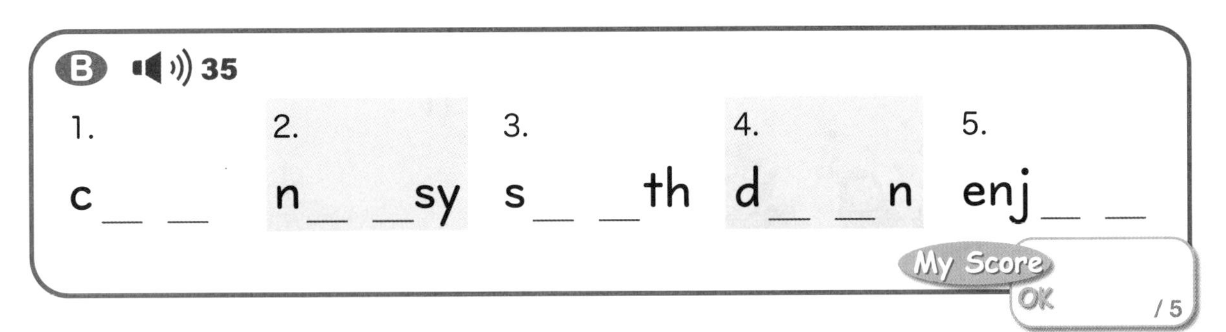

B 35
1. c__ __
2. n__ __sy
3. s__ __th
4. d__ __n
5. enj__ __
My Score
OK
/ 5

❶ Listening and Pointing 36

（文を聞いて指さし）

Listen to the story and point to the pictures.

（ストーリーを聞いて聞こえた単語の絵を指さそう。）

❷ Matching with Pictures（絵・文字合わせ）

Match the words with the pictures. Write the correct alphabet letters in the boxes.

（下の単語を声を出して読み、絵を左から選び、その記号を書こう。）

A B  C

D  E  F

G  H  I

J 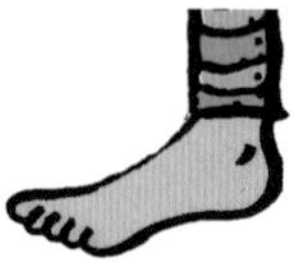 K  L

M  N  O

1. brown D
2. enjoy
3. nine
4. goat
5. mouth
6. foot
7. cook
8. elephant
9. blue
10. back
11. fish
12. eat

My Score OK / 12

❸ One Breath Game（一息ゲーム）

Say as many words as you can in one breath.
（一息でできるだけたくさん単語を言おう。）🔊 13

Take a deep breath. Ready, go!

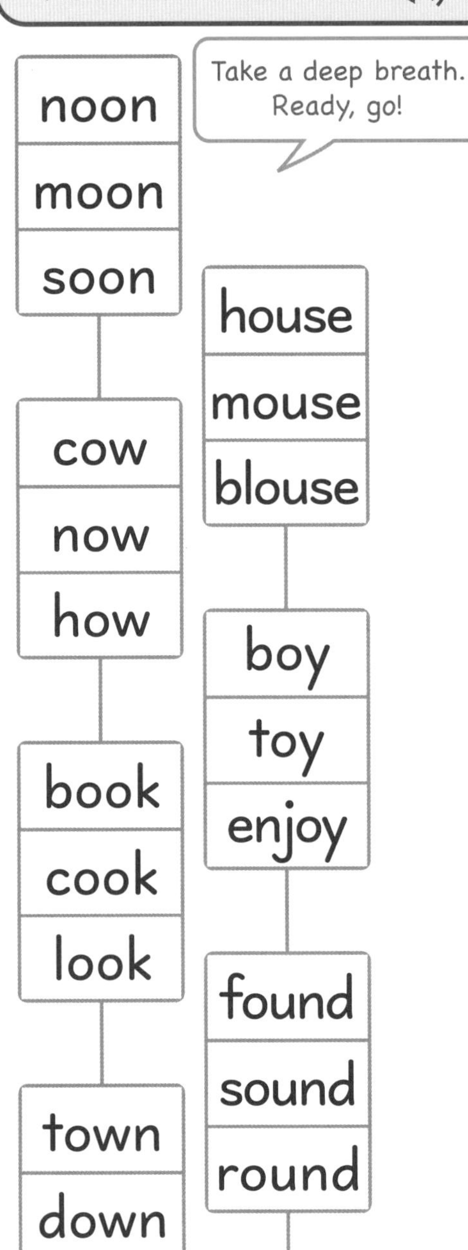

noon
moon
soon
house
mouse
blouse
cow
now
how
boy
toy
enjoy
book
cook
look
found
sound
round
town
down
brown
boil
coil
oil

❹ Grouping（仲間集め）

Find the 6 vowel rules hidden in the pictures. Write the rule numbers and the words below.
（ルール文字を見つけて番号を入れ、絵の単語を書こう。）

❶

あっ、丸い家だ！

❷
本を見なきゃ料理はできない

❸

ジャラジャラ、コインがうるさい

❹

牛が街を歩いているよ！

❺

男の子が楽しんでいるね

❻

じゃ、お昼にプールで

番号	ルール	単語	
2	oo	book	
	oo		
	ou		
	ow		
	oi		
	oy		

Wrap-up まとめと練習

Check the boxes after reading the words.
単語が読めたらチェックしよう。

Review ワークブックに出てきた単語
Challenge 1 / Challenge 2 読めるかどうか、チャレンジしてみる語句・文

Review

1	☐ blouse	8	☐ cook	15	☐ house	22	☐ noon	29	☐ sound
2	☐ boil	9	☐ cow	16	☐ how	23	☐ now	30	☐ south
3	☐ book	10	☐ down	17	☐ look	24	☐ oil	31	☐ town
4	☐ boy	11	☐ enjoy	18	☐ moon	25	☐ pool	32	☐ toy
5	☐ brown	12	☐ food	19	☐ mouse	26	☐ room		
6	☐ coil	13	☐ foot	20	☐ mouth	27	☐ round		
7	☐ coin	14	☐ found	21	☐ noisy	28	☐ soon		

Challenge 1

1	☐ about	7	☐ football	13	☐ noodle	19	☐ rookie	25	☐ took
2	☐ around	8	☐ good	14	☐ oops	20	☐ sauce	26	☐ tooth
3	☐ August	9	☐ hawk	15	☐ out	21	☐ saw	27	☐ voice
4	☐ choose	10	☐ jaw	16	☐ outside	22	☐ seafood	28	☐ without
5	☐ cool	11	☐ join	17	☐ owl	23	☐ straw	29	☐ wow
6	☐ count	12	☐ joy	18	☐ Paul	24	☐ thousand	30	☐ zookeeper

Challenge 2

1	☐ a bamboo box	7	☐ Enjoy your seafood.
2	☐ a big yawn	8	☐ Good luck!
3	☐ a cowboy	9	☐ I put on a brown blouse.
4	☐ a ten yen coin	10	☐ It is hot in August.
5	☐ a thick book	11	☐ Nice to meet you, too.
6	☐ A cow is in the town.	12	☐ Please wait at a pool.

65 のルール以外で、英語を読む時に役立つ読み方を紹介するよ！

6 oo と同じ音の u

rule
ルール

u は Rule 49 room の oo と同じ音。

1. rule ルール　2. flute フルート　3. supermarket スーパーマーケット　4. rude 不作法な

push
押す

u は Rule 50 book の oo と同じ音。

5. push 押す　6. pull 引く　7. put 置く　8. pudding プリン　9. full 十分な

Let's Read!

□put　□supermarket　□pudding　□flute　□push
□rule　□full　□rude　□pull

♪ Let's Chant!　37
チャンツに合わせて読んでみよう。

「○○って〜みたい！」と言いたい時に使えるフレーズです。

Just like something 〈まるで〜みたい！〉

*As strong as an ox,
As sly as a fox,
As fat as a pig,
As big as a whale,
＊くり返し
As quiet as a mouse,
As fast as a cheetah,
As cold as ice,

As hot as the sun,
As dry as a bone,
As thin as paper,
As loyal as a dog,
As cute as a kitten,
As free as a bird,
As cool as a cucumber.

意味

雄牛みたいに強い
キツネみたいにずるい
ブタみたいに太ってる
クジラみたいに大きい
ネズミみたいに静か
チーターみたいに速い
氷みたいに冷たい

太陽みたいに熱い
骨みたいにカラカラ
紙みたいにうすい
犬みたいに忠実
子猫みたいにかわいい
小鳥みたいに自由
きゅうりみたいにひんやり

『I like coffee, I like tea』より

65 のルール以外で、英語を読む時に役立つ読み方を紹介するよ！

7 子音が 2 つあっても 1 つしか読まない

1つしか読まない
rabbit
うさぎ

子音が2つあっても
1つしか読まない。

bb	ll	mm	ss	pp
1. rabbit うさぎ	3. bell ベル	5. summer 夏	7. dress ドレス	9. apple りんご
2. bubble あわ	4. tell 話す	6. grammar 文法	8. chess チェス	10. happy 幸せ

Let's Read!
☐happy ☐grammar ☐rabbit ☐tell ☐chess
☐summer ☐dress ☐apple ☐bubble ☐bell

8 au/aw と同じ音

au/awと同じ音
walk
歩く

au/awと同じ音
all
すべて

al と all どちらも au/awと同じ音。

1. walk 歩く 2. talk 話す 3. chalk チョーク

4. all すべて 5. ball ボール 6. tall 背が高い 7. fall 秋・落ちる 8. small 小さい

Let's Read!
☐small ☐talk ☐tall ☐chalk ☐fall ☐walk ☐ball ☐all

9 u の音読みする母音

uの音読み
come
来る

uの音読み
young
若い

o と ou どちらも uの音読み。

1. come 来る 2. some いくつかの 3. love 愛する 4. mother お母さん 5. son 息子

6. young 若い 7. cousin いとこ 8. country 国 9. touch さわる

Let's Read!
☐cousin ☐love ☐come ☐country ☐son
☐touch ☐some ☐young ☐mother

8. Consonant Blends （連続子音）

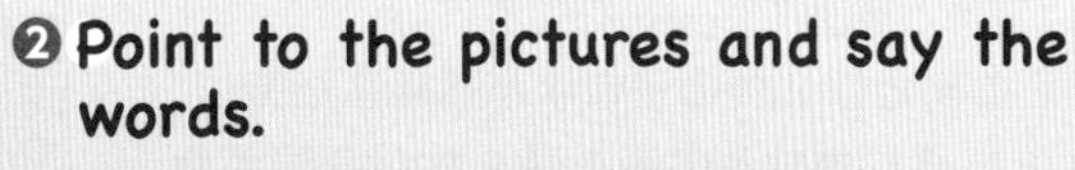

もう知っている言葉がたくさんあるね。

Vocabulary （単語） 38

❶ Listen and memorize the keywords.
（単語を聞いて覚えよう。）

❷ Point to the pictures and say the words.
（言いながら絵を指さそう。単語を言おう。）

1 
2 
3 
4 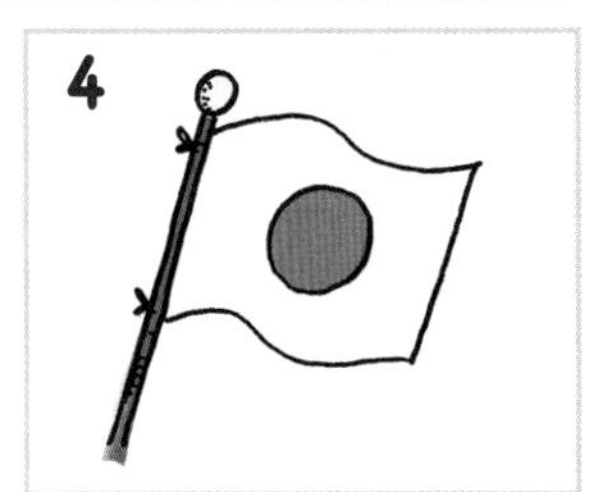

5 
6 
7 
8 

9 
10 
11 
12 

13 
14 
15 
16 

17 
18 
19 
20 

1 black	2 class	3 clock	4 flag
5 green	6 drink	7 drive	8 French
9 skate	10 stamp	11 slow	12 smile
13 snake	14 swim	15 tree	16 train
17 spring	18 street	19 three	20 throw

8. Consonant Blends

▶（連続子音）

❶ Rules 55 - 59 🔊 39

（音声と動画でルールを知ろう。）

2 つまたは 3 つの子音字が連続した時に、それぞれがもとの音を残しながら混ざりあった音になる。

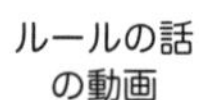

❷ Phonics Jingle 🔊 40

（ラップでルールを練習しよう。）

55
bl
b と l をつなげて早く

56
gr
g と r をつなげて早く

❸ Break down the word.

（単語の音を 1 音ごとに分けよう。）

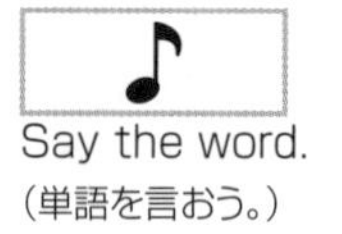

Say the word.
（単語を言おう。）

Break into sounds.
（1 音ごとに分けて□に書こう。）

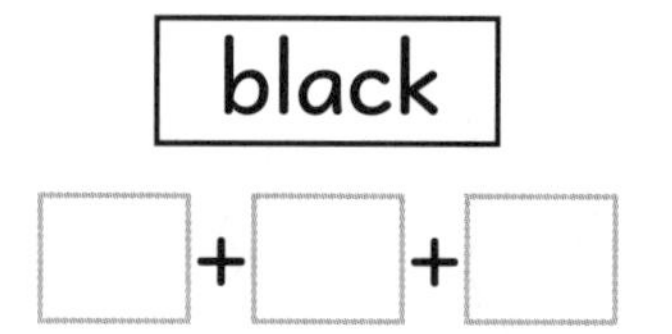

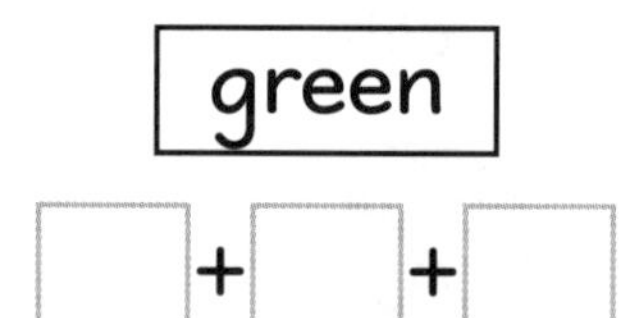

How many letters?
How many sounds?

❹ Read the word list on p. 43.

（43 ページの単語を読もう。）

❺ Listen and fill in the blanks.

（音声を聞いて、空所に文字を入れよう。）

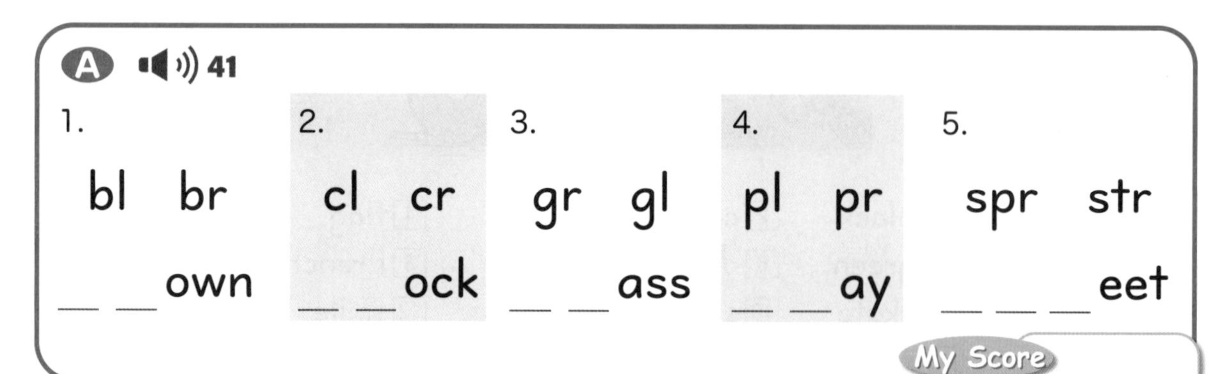

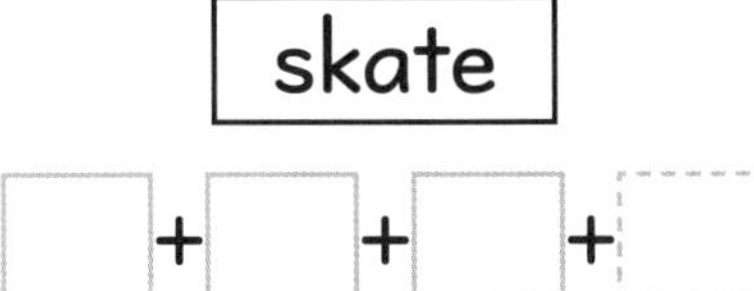

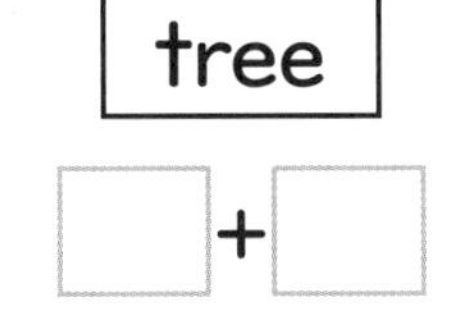

cl fl gl pl sl　　br cr dr fr

sm sn sp st sw　　str thr

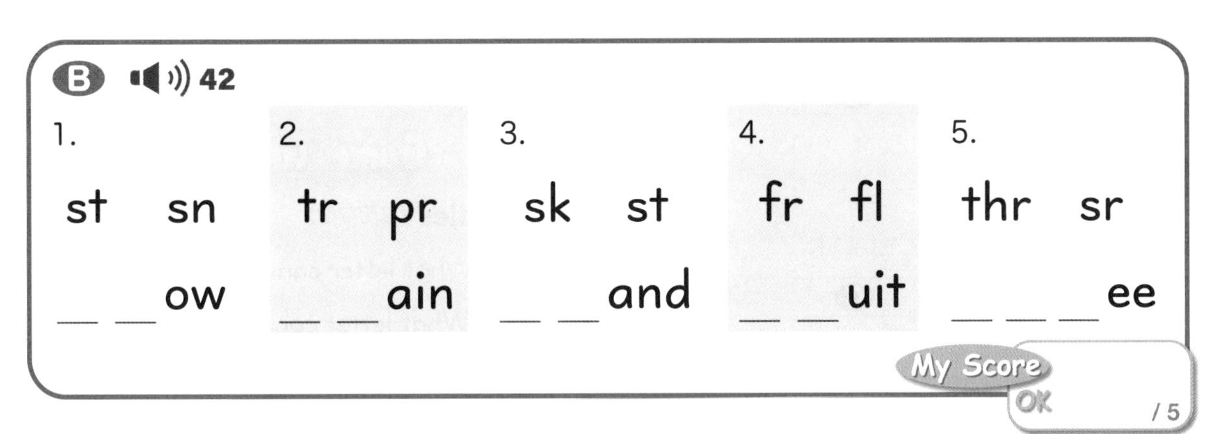

B 42
1. st sn __ __ ow
2. tr pr __ __ ain
3. sk st __ __ and
4. fr fl __ __ uit
5. thr sr __ __ __ ee
My Score OK /5

❶ One Finger, Two Fingers（指 1 本、指 2 本?）

Listen to the words. If you think it is No. 1, hold up one finger. If it is No. 2, hold up two fingers. Write 1 or 2 for the final quiz.
（単語を聞いて指 1 本か 2 本で答えよう。最後のクイズは 1 か 2 を書こう。）

43

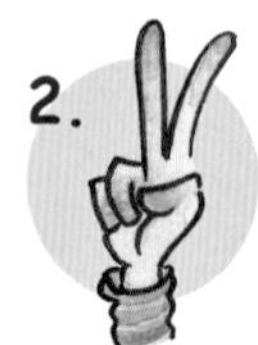

A 1. The grass is green.

2. The glass is green.

B 1. Let's play.

2. Let's pray.

C 1. I see a tree.

2. I see a three.

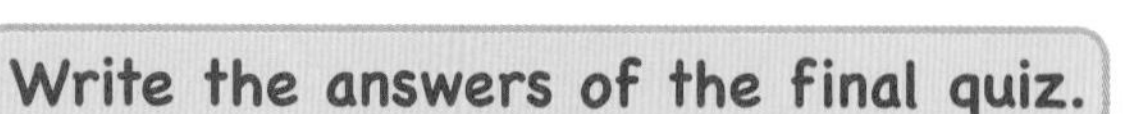

A	B	C

もう一度、チャレンジしてもいいよ。

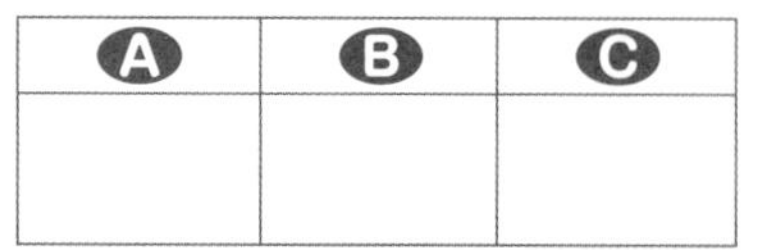

A	B	C

❷ Q and A Relay（QA リレー）

Answer, "Yes" or "No."
（質問リレーしよう。答えは"Yes"か"No"で。）

Yes! No!

1. Can a fish swim?
2. Can a frog jump?
3. Can a snake skip?
4. Can a whale sing?
5. Can a fox sit?
6. Can an elephant read?
7. Can a monkey drive?
8. Can a tree smile?

Riddles（なぞなぞ）

Q1: What letter can you drink?

Q2: What letter can see?

Q3: What letter stings you?

❸ Three Hints Game（3ヒントゲーム）

Read the 3 hints and race to answer.
（3ヒントを読んで早く答えよう。）

❹ Write the answers.

（3ヒントゲームの答えを書こう。）

Ⓐ cow, white, drink

Ⓑ big, animal, sea

Ⓒ food, eat, noon

Ⓓ hot, shampoo, soap

Ⓔ no legs, long, eats frogs

Ⓕ read, page, story

Ⓖ mail, send, card

Ⓗ ice, sport, shoes

Ⓐ ____________

Ⓑ ____________

Ⓒ ____________

Ⓓ ____________

Ⓔ ____________

Ⓕ ____________

Ⓖ ____________

Ⓗ ____________

My Score OK /8

問題を作って友だちと遊ぼう。

❶

❷

❸

Wrap-up まとめと練習

Check the boxes after reading the words.
単語が読めたらチェックしよう。

Review ワークブックに出てきた単語
Challenge 1 / Challenge 2 読めるかどうか、チャレンジしてみる語句・文

Review

1 animal
2 black
3 class
4 clock
5 drink
6 drive
7 flag
8 French
9 frog
10 glass
11 grass
12 green
13 ice
14 jump
15 mail
16 milk
17 page
18 pray
19 send
20 shampoo
21 shoe(s)
22 skate
23 skip
24 slow
25 smile
26 snake
27 soap
28 spring
29 stamp
30 stand(up)
31 story
32 street
33 swim
34 three
35 throw
36 train
37 tree

Challenge 1

1 blanket
2 block
3 blog
4 blond
5 bring
6 brush
7 chopstick
8 classmate
9 classroom
10 crab
11 crane
12 cross
13 crowd
14 drama
15 drop
16 drum
17 flute
18 fresh
19 globe
20 plane
21 planet
22 plant
23 plastic
24 project
25 slice
26 smoke
27 snack
28 snap
29 Spain
30 spoon
31 spray
32 staff
33 step
34 sting
35 strong
36 study
37 throat
38 trash
39 trick
40 trip
41 trumpet

Challenge 2

1 a big smile
2 a Japanese flag
3 a light snack
4 a long snake
5 a plastic bag
6 a slow bus
7 a sweet cake
8 French food
9 fresh fruit
10 juice in a glass
11 I like Spain.
12 I sleep in a bed.
13 We drink green tea.
14 You swim in the sea.

9. Murmuring Vowels

（R のついた母音）

今度はどんなルールかな？

Vocabulary （単語） 44

❶ Listen and memorize the keywords.
（単語を聞いて覚えよう。）

❷ Point to the pictures and say the words.
（言いながら絵を指さそう。単語を言おう。）

1

2

3

4

5

6
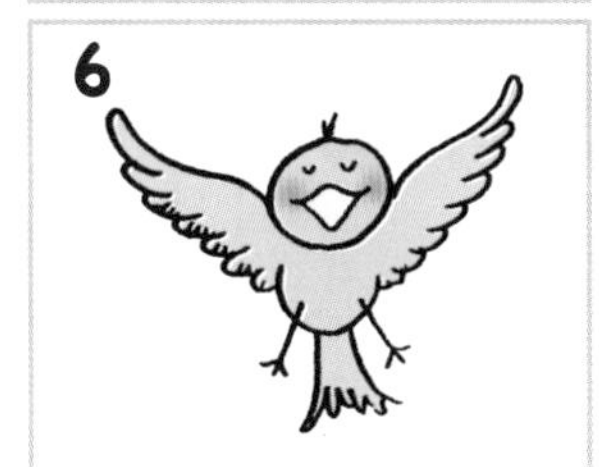

7

8

9

10

11
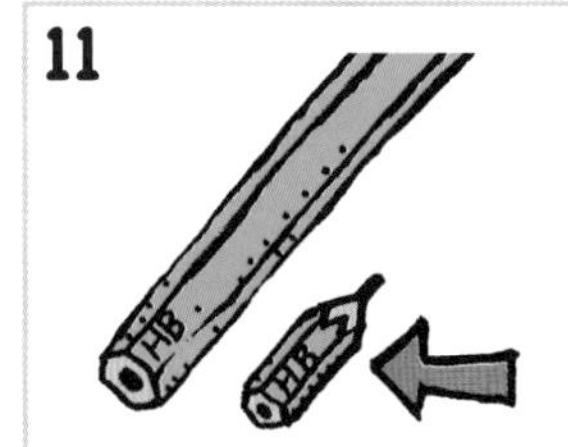

12

13
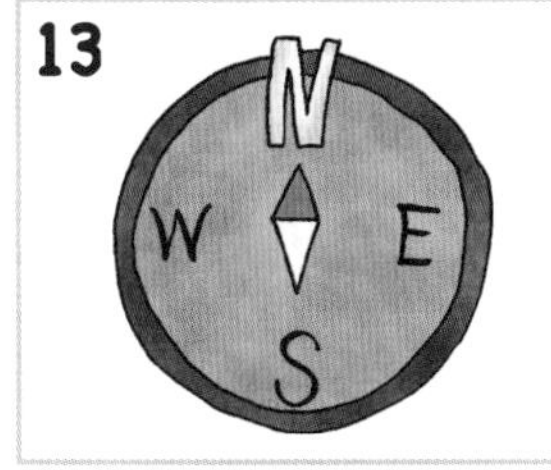

14

15

16
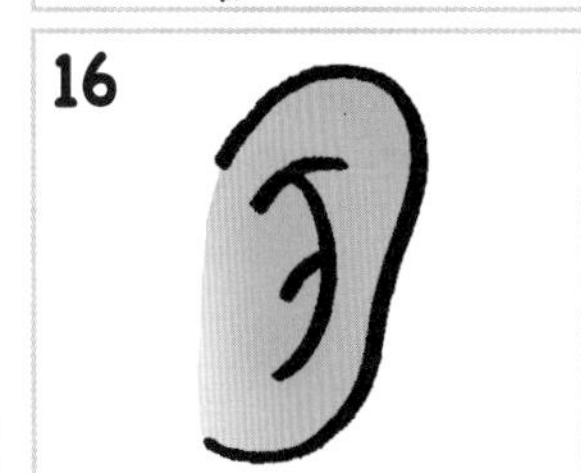

17

18

19

20

1 car	2 star	3 park	4 March
5 girl	6 bird	7 birthday	8 first
9 word	10 work	11 short	12 sport
13 north	14 fork	15 hear	16 ear
17 year	18 flower	19 teacher	20 winter

9. Murmuring Vowels

▶（Rのついた母音）

❶ Rules 60 - 65 45

（音声と動画でルールを知ろう。）

母音に r がつくと、混合された新しい音になる。あいまいな音になるので「あいまい母音」とも言う。この音がうまく出せたら達人。

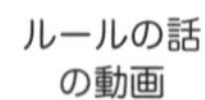

❷ Phonics Jingle 46

（ラップでルールを練習しよう。）

❸ Break down the word.

（単語の音を1音ごとに分けよう。）

Say the word.

（単語を言おう。）

Break into sounds.

（1音ごとに分けて□に書こう。）

❹ Read the word list on p. 49.

（49ページの単語を読もう。）

❺ Listen and fill in the blanks.

（音声を聞いて、空所に文字を入れよう。）

car

□ + □

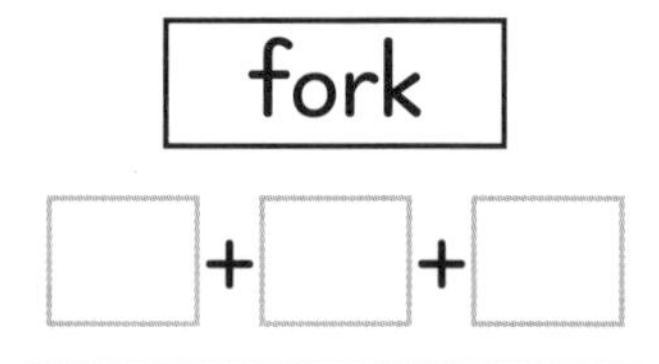

□ + □ + □

64
ear
i の音と _e r の音をつなげて

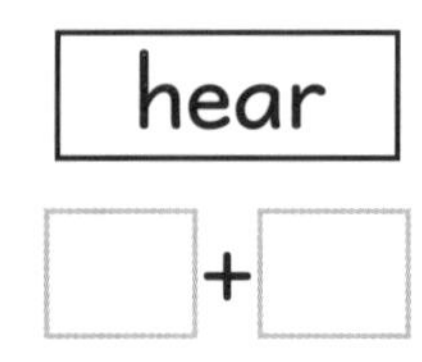

□ + □

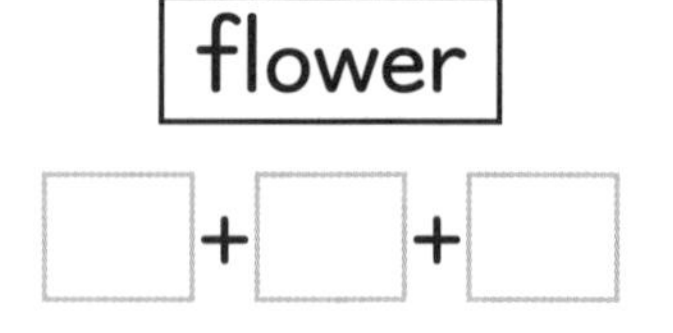

□ + □ + □

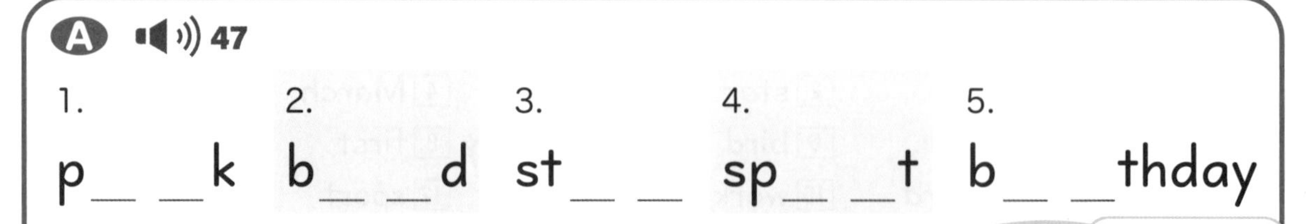

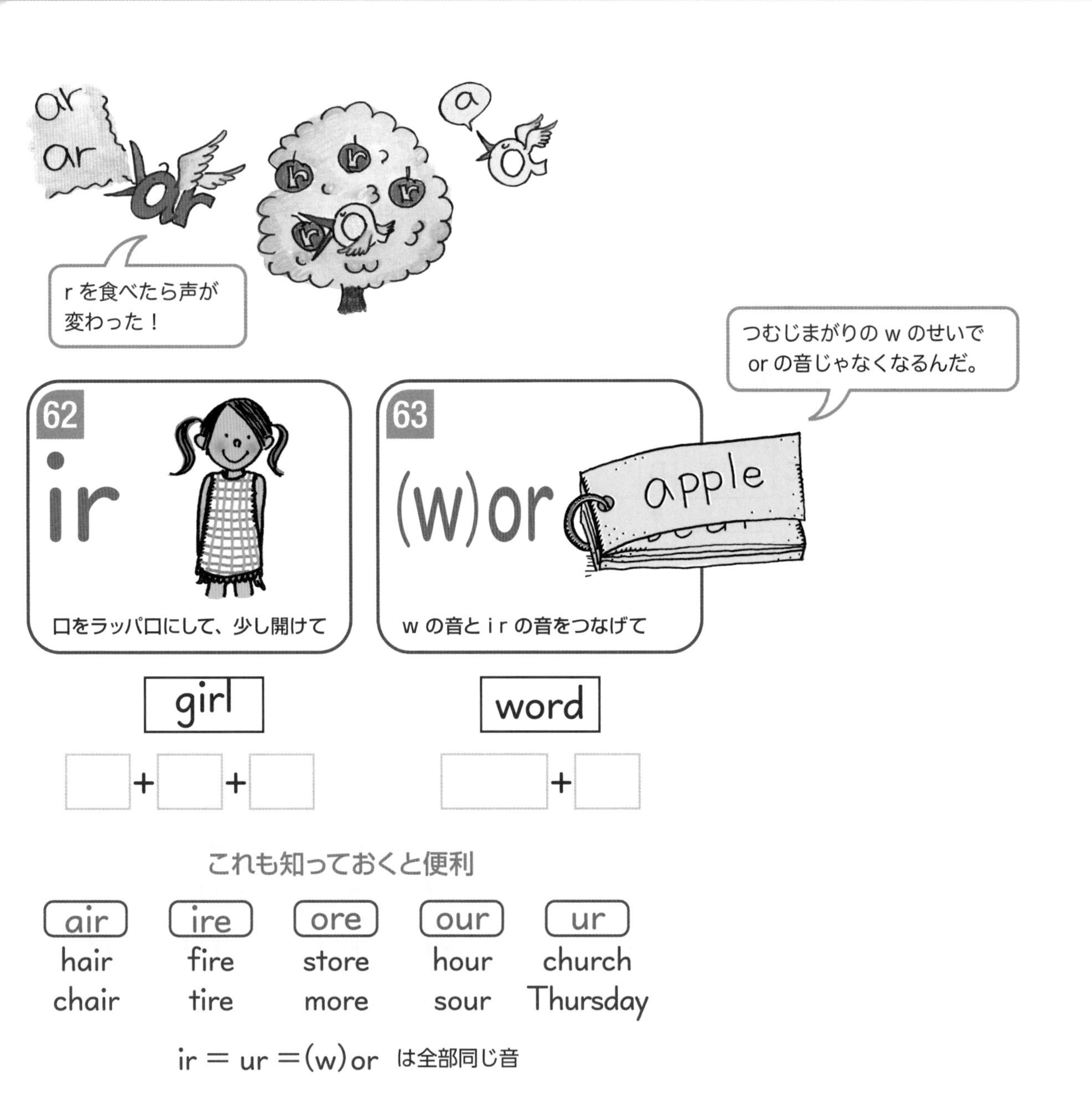
ar
ar
ar
a
r を食べたら声が
変わった！
つむじまがりの w のせいで
or の音じゃなくなるんだ。
62
ir
口をラッパ口にして、少し開けて
63
(w)or
apple
w の音と i r の音をつなげて
girl
word
□ + □ + □
□ + □
これも知っておくと便利
air
hair
chair
ire
fire
tire
ore
store
more
our
hour
sour
ur
church
Thursday
ir ＝ ur ＝(w)or は全部同じ音

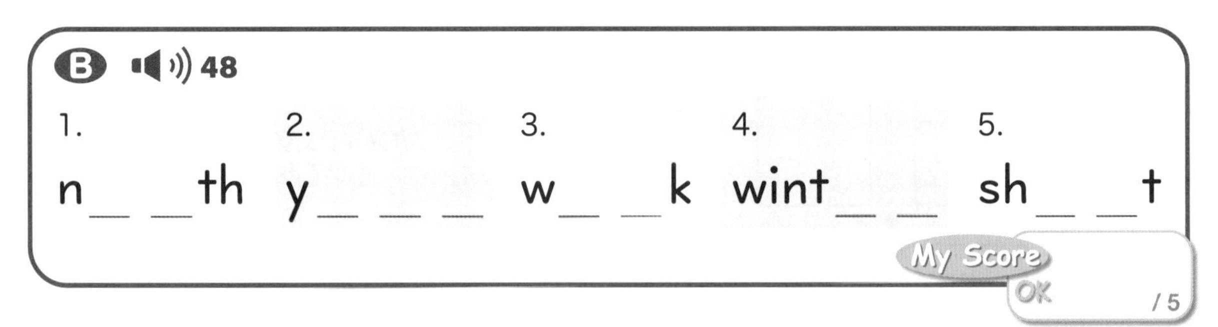
B 48
1. n_ _th
2. y_ _ _
3. w_ _k
4. wint_ _
5. sh_ _t
My Score
OK
/ 5

❶ Driving Game（運転ゲーム）

Listen to the words. If you hear "ar" sound, drive to your left. If you hear "or" sound, go straight. If you hear "ir" sound, drive to your right. Where are you now? Circle the letter.
（単語を聞いて、左折／直進／右折しよう。最後はどこにいるか○をつけよう。）

49

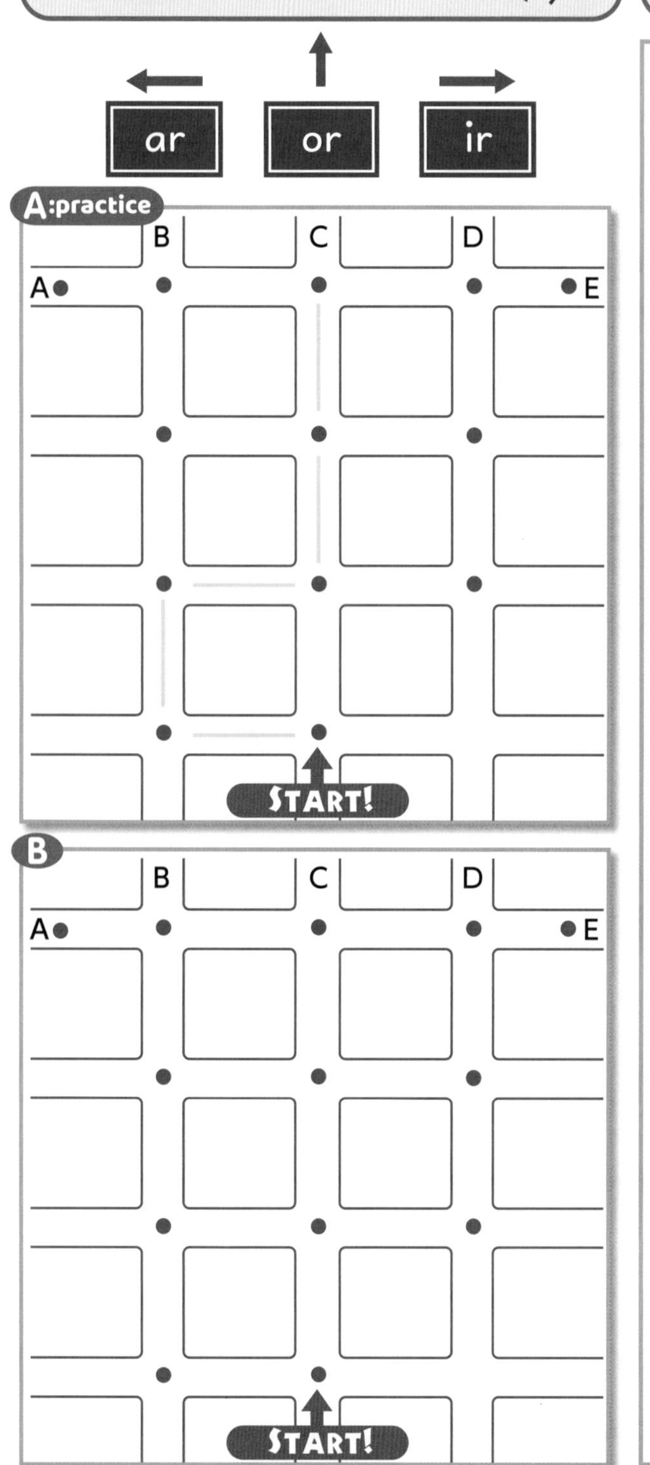

❷ Speed Reading Tennis（ペアで交代早読み）

13

In pairs, take turns reading the words. Student A reads the words in the white boxes. Student B reads the blue boxes.
（ペアで交代に単語を読もう。1 人は白いボックス、もう 1 人は青いボックスを読もう。）

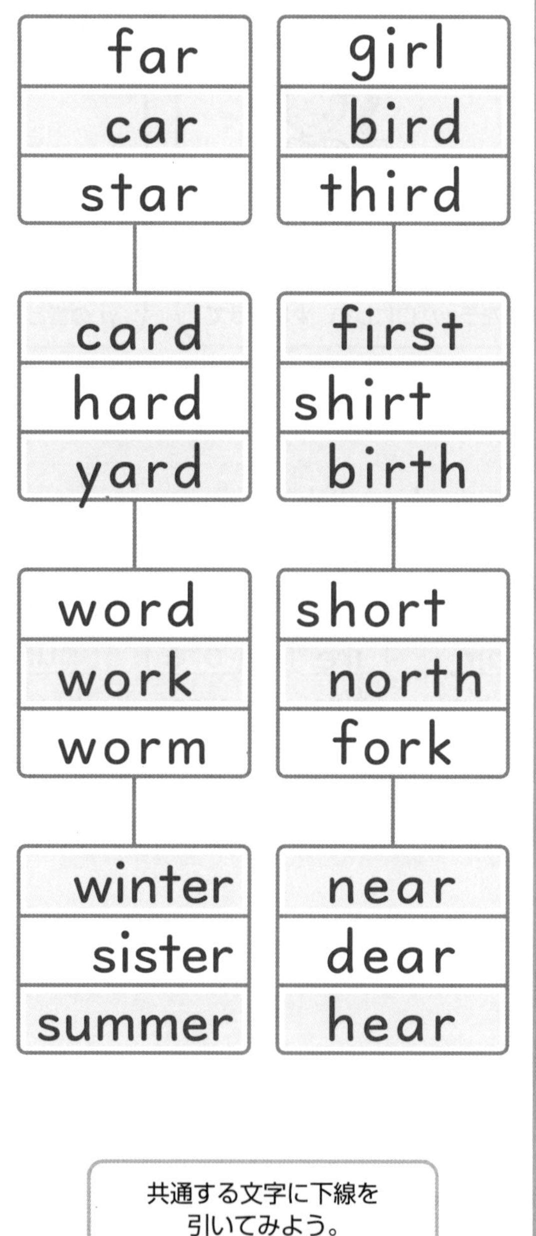

共通する文字に下線を引いてみよう。

❸ Secret Messages （秘密のメッセージ）

Guess the missing words from the pictures, and then write them. Read the secret message.
（メッセージを読もう。下線に単語を書こう。）

1 and 2 a 3 .

1. ________ ____ 2. ________

3. ________

Open your mouth. 4 at your left 5

and then touch your 6 .

4. ________ 5. ________ 6. ________

Say when your 7 is. 8 a happy song.

7. ________ 8. ________

9 a ball to a classmate and 10 .

9. ________ 10. ____ ________

My Score OK / 10

❹ Find the partner

（パートナー探し）

Read the words, and then write the paired words from the hints.
（単語を読んでヒントから対になっている単語を選んで書こう。）

1. long ________
2. boy ________
3. good ________
4. fast ________
5. queen ________

Hints

white	bad
king	sit
slow	girl
short	spoon

My Score OK / 5

Wrap-up まとめと練習

Check the boxes after reading the words.
単語が読めたらチェックしよう。

Review ワークブックに出てきた単語
Challenge 1 / Challenge 2 読めるかどうか、チャレンジしてみる語句・文

Review

1 ☐ bird
2 ☐ birth
3 ☐ birthday
4 ☐ car
5 ☐ card
6 ☐ dear
7 ☐ ear
8 ☐ far
9 ☐ first
10 ☐ flower
11 ☐ fork
12 ☐ girl
13 ☐ hard
14 ☐ hear
15 ☐ March
16 ☐ near
17 ☐ north
18 ☐ park
19 ☐ shirt
20 ☐ short
21 ☐ sister
22 ☐ sport
23 ☐ star
24 ☐ summer
25 ☐ teacher
26 ☐ third
27 ☐ winter
28 ☐ word
29 ☐ work
30 ☐ worm
31 ☐ yard
32 ☐ year

Challenge 1

1 ☐ actor
2 ☐ arm
3 ☐ art
4 ☐ artist
5 ☐ baker
6 ☐ chair
7 ☐ church
8 ☐ corn
9 ☐ fire
10 ☐ hair
11 ☐ horse
12 ☐ hour
13 ☐ large
14 ☐ market
15 ☐ more
16 ☐ morning
17 ☐ number
18 ☐ October
19 ☐ party
20 ☐ passport
21 ☐ pork
22 ☐ sour
23 ☐ start
24 ☐ store
25 ☐ thirsty
26 ☐ thirteen
27 ☐ thirty
28 ☐ Thursday
29 ☐ tire
30 ☐ turtle

Challenge 2

1 ☐ a big bird nest
2 ☐ a birthday cake in a box
3 ☐ as cool as a cucumber
4 ☐ black and white
5 ☐ the moon and a star
6 ☐ World Cup
7 ☐ Are you a good singer?
8 ☐ Are you tired?
9 ☐ Can I have a sticker?
10 ☐ He made a sharp turn to the left.
11 ☐ I don't like a sour taste.
12 ☐ I go to a department store.
13 ☐ I'm thirsty.
14 ☐ It's my turn.
15 ☐ Look at your left arm.
16 ☐ My birthday is in March.
17 ☐ That girl is a good dancer.
18 ☐ That's not fair.
19 ☐ The trees turn red in fall.
20 ☐ Turn right at the corner.

10. Plurals

（複数形）

名詞につく「しっぽの s」の音

❶Read the words. Fold the page on the broken line.
（単語を読もう。点線で谷折りしよう。） 50

1. 音は s
無声音で終わる単語につく s

cup
map
cat

2. 音は z
有声音で終わる単語につく s

pen
hand
key

おまけ
baby （赤ちゃん）
leaf （葉）

3. 音は iz
s, z, ch, sh, x 等の音で終わる単語につく s/es

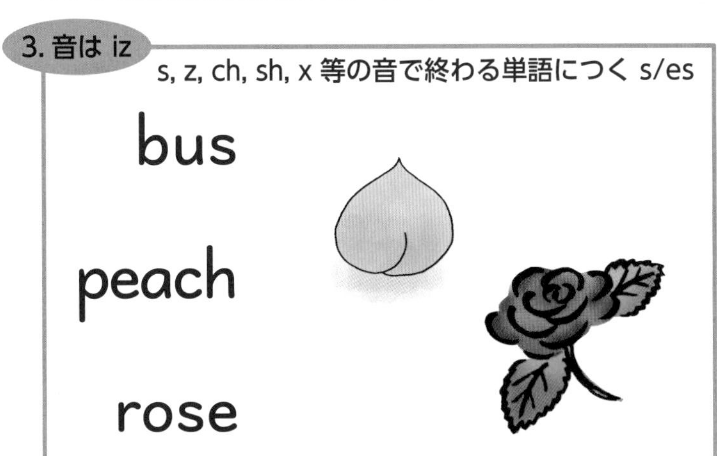

bus
peach
rose

谷折り

❷In pairs, say the words. Partners say the plural forms.
（ペアで 1 人が単語、もう 1 人は複数形を言おう。）

1. elephant
2. bag
3. cherry
4. day
5. knife
6. bird
7. box
8. dish
9. ship

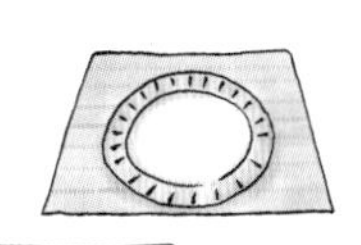

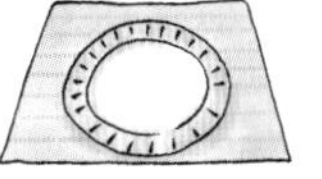

英語では、単語を言う時、それが 1つなのか 2 つ以上なのかをきちんと区別する。ネコが 1 匹なら 'a cat'、2 匹なら 'two cats'。「しっぽの s」が 2 つ以上のマーク。「しっぽの s」の音は、3 種類。どの音になるかは、単語の終わりの音が決め手。

Fold the page on the broken line. Say the words in plural forms.
（線で山折りして、単語の複数形を言おう。）

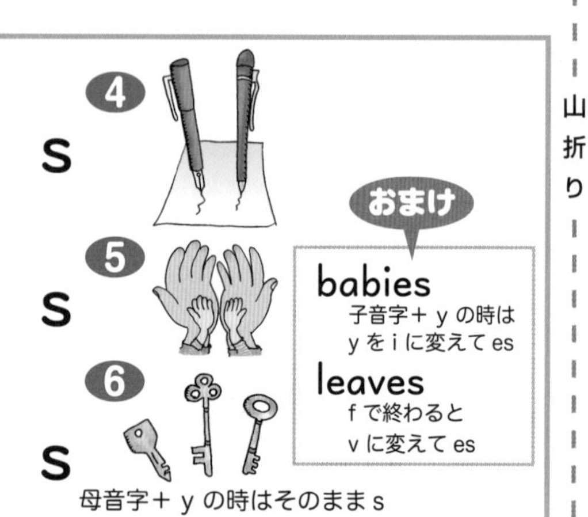

4 s
5 s
6 s
母音字＋ y の時はそのまま s
おまけ
babies
子音字＋ y の時は
y を i に変えて es
leaves
f で終わると
v に変えて es

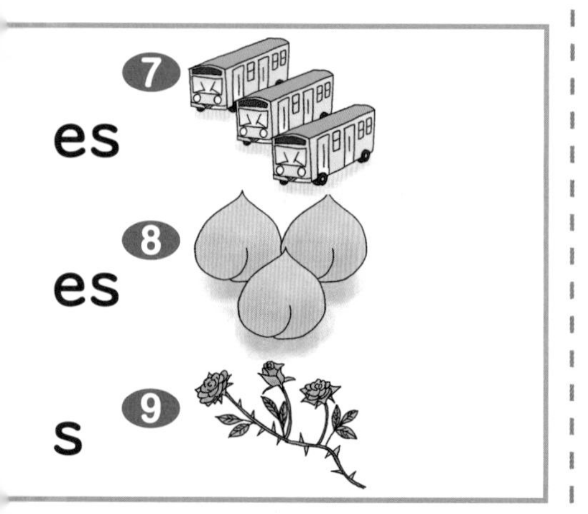

山折り

❸ Look at the pictures on the left and write the answers.
（左の絵を見て、下線に答えを書こう。）

What are these?

1. These are c u p s.
2. These are _ _ _ _.
3. ______________________.
4. ______________________.
5. ______________________.
6. ______________________.

What are those?

7. Those are ______________.
8. ______________________.
9. ______________________.

Game Time!

One Finger, Two Fingers （指１本、指２本？）

リーダーが❶～❾のイラストからひとつ単語を選んで、シャウト！単数形だったら指１本、複数形だったら指２本で答えよう。

cups!

④ Write your own answers.
(質問に答えよう。)

❶ How many noses do you have?

I have ____________________

❷ How many pens do you have?

I have ____________________

❸ How many legs does a bird have?

It has ____________________

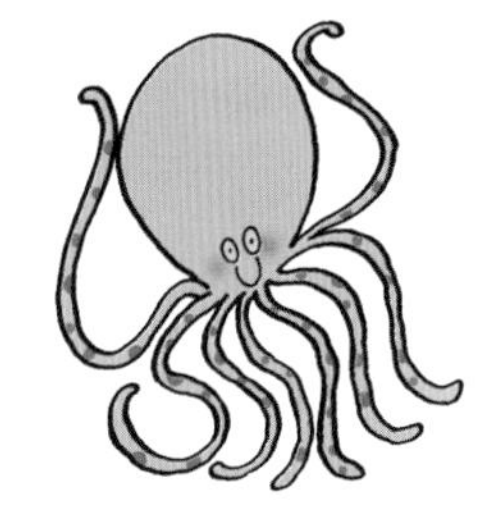

❹ How many legs does a cow have?

It has ____________________

❺ How many legs does an octopus have?

It has ____________________

❻ How many legs does a snake have?

It has ____________________

❼ How many windows are there in this room?

There are ____________________

❽ How many books do you have in your bag?

I have ____________________

zero(no), one, two, three, four, five, six, seven, eight, nine, ten

11. Third Person Singular S （3人称単数現在のS）

動詞につく「しっぽの s」の音

3人称単数現在形の s のつけ方は名詞に s をつけた時と同じで、
単語の最後の音によって変わります。

		主語	動詞の現在形
1人称	単数	I（私は）	jump.
	複数	We（私たちは）	jump.
2人称	単数	You（あなたは）	jump.
	複数	You（あなたたちは）	jump.
3人称	単数	He（= Ted, My father, etc.）（彼は） She（= Meg, My mother, etc.）（彼女は） It（= The cat, etc.）（それは）	jumps.
	複数	They（彼らは）	jump.

❶ Read the words.
（単語を読もう。） 51

jump – jumps

1. 音は s

jumps ・・・ ジャンプする
helps ・・・ 助ける
likes ・・・ 好き
looks ・・・ 見る
works ・・・ 働く

starts ・・・ スタートする
wants ・・・ ほしい
hits ・・・ 打つ
sits ・・・ すわる
eats ・・・ 食べる

play – plays

（母音字 + y なら そのまま s）

2. 音は z

plays ・・・ 遊ぶ
enjoys ・・・ 楽しむ
sings ・・・ 歌う
swims ・・・ 泳ぐ
runs ・・・ 走る

cry – cries

（子音字 + y なら y を i に変える）

fly–flies ・・・ 飛ぶ
study–studies ・・・ 勉強する
go–goes ・・・ 行く
do–does ・・・ する

read – reads

reads ・・・ 読む
needs ・・・ 必要とする
ends ・・・ 終わる

wash – washes

3. 音は iz

passes ・・・ 通る
mixes ・・・ 混ぜる
washes ・・・ 洗う
teaches ・・・ 教える
uses ・・・ 使う

❷ Fill in the blanks.
（あてはまる単語を書こう。）

1. I like dogs. Ted __________ dogs, too.
2. I eat peaches. Meg __________ peaches, too.
3. I wash my face. The cat __________ its face, too.
4. I enjoy music. My mom __________ music, too.
5. I read books. My dad __________ books, too.
6. I sometimes cry. The baby often __________ .
7. I study English. Tim __________ Spanish.
8. I brush my teeth. My sister __________ her teeth, too.
9. I want cake. But, my sisters __________ pie.
10. I play games. My mom and dad __________ games, too.

My Score
OK / 10

12. Past Tense ▶(過去形)

動詞につく「しっぽの ed」の音

もう終わったことや、前にそうだったことを「過去」という。大部分の動詞は ed のしっぽをつけると過去形になる。しっぽの ed を音で分けた３タイプについて勉強しよう。しっぽがつかずに形が変わってしまう「不規則動詞」は何度も言って覚えよう。

❶ **Read the words.**
(単語を読もう。) 52

jump – jumped

1. 音は t

jumped ・・・ ジャンプした
helped ・・・ 助けた
looked ・・・ 見た
washed ・・・ 洗った
walked ・・・ 歩いた

stop – stopped
(短母音 + 子音の時、子音を重ねる)

stopped ・・・ ストップした
skipped ・・・ スキップした

play – played
(母音字 + y ならそのまま ed)

2. 音は d

played ・・・ 遊んだ
enjoyed ・・・ 楽しんだ
stayed ・・・ 泊まった
pulled ・・・ 引っぱった
used ・・・ 使った

cry – cried
(子音字 + y なら y を i に変える)

cry–cried ・・・ 泣いた
dry–dried ・・・ 乾かした
study–studied ・・・ 勉強した

start – started

3. 音は id

started ・・・ スタートした
wanted ・・・ ほしかった
waited ・・・ 待った
needed ・・・ 必要だった
ended ・・・ 終わった

不規則動詞

sit – sat ・・・ すわった
run – ran ・・・ 走った
sing – sang ・・・ 歌った
swim – swam ・・・ 泳いだ

come – came ・・・ 来た
eat – ate ・・・ 食べた
hit – hit ・・・ 打った
read – read ・・・ 読んだ
(発音に注意)

go – went ・・・ 行った
teach – taught ・・・ 教えた
fly – flew ・・・ 飛んだ
buy – bought ・・・ 買った

❷ Fill in the blanks.
（60ページの動詞を補って、日記を完成させよう。）

Sunday, March 20

At six I ❶ ________ my face. I ❷ ________ with my dog.
My dog ❸ ________ off my cap. I ❹ ________ hotdogs for lunch.
In the afternoon, I ❺ ________ shopping. I ❻ ________ a notebook.
I ❼ ________ English at night. I ❽ ________ music.
I ❾ ________ to bed at nine. Good night.

My Score
OK /9

❸ Write your own diary.
（自分の日記を3文書こう。）

❶ ________

❷ ________

❸ ________

母音グループ

1文字1音グループ

Phonics Alphabet (フォニックスアルファベット)

1 a : apple 5 e : egg 9 i : ink 15 o : octopus 21 u : umbrella

Short Vowels (5 つの短母音)

1 a : bag cat hat jam man
5 e : bed men pen red ten
9 i : big pig pin sit six
15 o : box hot mom stop top
21 u : bus cup cut run sun

名前読みの母音グループ

Silent E (E のついた母音)

27 a–e : cake game lake name
28 e–e : Eve he Pete we
29 i–e : bike five nine time
30 o–e : home nose pole rose
31 u–e : cube cute June tube

Polite Vowels (礼儀正しい母音)

32 ai : rain wait
33 ay : day May play
34 ea : eat read tea
35 ee : sleep week
36 ie : pie tie
37 oa : boat road
38 ow : snow window
39 ue : blue glue
40 ui : fruit juice

2文字で新しい音グループ

Vowel Digraphs (2 文字母音)

49 oo : food noon pool room
50 oo : book cook foot look
51 ou : house mouth round south
52 ow : brown cow down town
53 oi : coin noisy
54 oy : boy enjoy

混ざりあった音グループ

Murmuring Vowels (R のついた母音)

60 ar : car March park star
61 or : fork north short sport
62 ir : bird birthday first girl
63 (w)or : word work
64 ear : ear hear year
65 _er : flower teacher winter

子音グループ

1文字1音グループ

Phonics Alphabet (フォニックスアルファベット)

2 b : bear
3 c : cow
4 d : dog
6 f : fish
7 g : goat
8 h : hat
10 j : jet
11 k : king
12 l : lion
13 m : monkey
14 n : nest
16 p : pig
17 q : queen
18 r : rabbit
19 s : sun
20 t : tiger
22 v : violin
23 w : witch
24 x : fox
25 y : yard
26 z : zebra

2文字で新しい音グループ

Consonant Digraphs (2文字子音)

41 ch : chime lunch teach
42 sh : dish fish ship
43 ph : elephant phone
44 wh : whale white
45 th : math think
46 th : that these this those
47 ck : back rock
48 ng : long sing

混ざりあった音グループ

Consonant Blends (連続子音)

55 bl : black / cl : class clock / fl : flag
56 gr : green / dr : drink drive / fr : French
57 sk : skate / sl : slow / sm : smile
sn : snake / st : stamp / sw : swim
58 tr : train tree
59 spr : spring / str : street / thr : three throw

New Active Phonics

発行日　2001年12月 1日　初版　第1刷
　　　　2023年11月20日　第2版第2刷

著　　　者 ● 松香洋子、宮清子、樋田 禎美
執 筆 協 力 ● 本多敏幸、粕谷みゆき、近藤佐知子、山下千里、伊藤美幸、近藤理恵子
Beth Castillo、Damien Pratt、Suzy Nachtsheim
イ ラ ス ト ● 堀その子
表　　　紙 ● 柿沼みさと
本文デザイン・組版 ● Taira Design
編　　　集 ● 株式会社エディット
印　　　刷 ● （株）大熊整美堂
ナレーション ● Walter Roberts、Minako "mooki" Obata
歌　　　唱 ● Andy Wulf、MICKEY-T.、Walter Roberts
音　　　楽 ● 住友紀人、鶴谷智生

発　　　行 ● 株式会社 mpi 松香フォニックス
〒151-0053　東京都渋谷区代々木 2-16-2 第二甲田ビル 2F　fax:03-5302-1652
URL:https://www.mpi-j.co.jp
株式会社正進社
〒112-0014　東京都文京区関口 1-17-8　phone:03-5229-7651
URL:https://www.seishinsha.co.jp

ISBN 978-4-89643-790-4

学校用教師指導書については
mpi 松香フォニックスへお問い合わせください。
E-mail：mpi@mpi-j.co.jp